Still Searching

For Our Identical, Triplet Sister

By Cheryl G. Kaye

Dedication

I am pleased to dedicate this book to my twin sister, Michelle as well as my family. Without their support, the "dead ends" and "rejections" would have been difficult to cope with.

Yes, there have been many leads. Yes, there are documents that have been illegally changed. Yes, there have been many sightings, told to us by people that we have both met.

I never thought it would take so long to locate an identical, triplet sister who was adopted out at the time of our births.

Our mother always asked us to never stop searching.

Hence, the reason for writing this book. <u>Still Searching</u>.

Published 2017

Copyright @ 2017 by Cheryl G. Kaye

All rights reserved

Designed by Cheryl G. Kaye

ISBN - 13: 978-1979256964

ISBN – 10: 1979256969

Our Parents – Jane and Stanley Gemalo   November 27, 1949

Contents

Cover Page	1
Dedication	2
Mom and Dad's wedding day - November 27, 1949	3
Contents	4/5
Searches	6/7
Synopsis	8
Important Facts	9
Mom's Verbal Story to us – 1963	10
In Search of our Triplet Sister, as Kids	11
Leap Frog	12/13
Questions, Questions, Questions	14/17
Mid-Island Shopping Plaza – We meet for the last time– 1963	18/19
Time Lapsed… into Years	20
Our Easter Vacation in Clearwater, Fl. My Lost Camera 1984-1985	21/23
Newspaper Article: Burglar Killed by Clearwater Police – 1985	24
Newspaper Article: Search – 1985	25
Clearwater Police Department – Detective Jim Gravely's Photos – 1985	26
What is a Coverslip Birth Certificate? Ocala, Fl. – 1985	27
Cheryl's Birth Certificate	28
Dr. Ryan's Letter to Our Mom Information – 1951	29
Dr. Ryan's Letter to Our Mom Original	30
Cheryl's Official Certificate of Birth with footprints from M.I.H.	31
Michelle's Official Certificate of Birth with footprints from M.I.H.	32
Receipt from Newton County Police Department-For Inking our Feet	33

In Short: Summary of Information	34/35
Left Foot – Cheryl	36
Right Foot – Cheryl	37
Left Foot – Michelle	38
Right Foot – Michelle	39
Photo of Us in Snowsuits	40
In Review- Discrepancies	41
Useful Information	42
In Search of a Private Investigator-1996	43/46
I Hired a Private Investigator – E-mails and Conversations – 1997	47/50
*Three Girls Born on January 15, 1951	51
Michelle's Birth Certificate Index Number 401017	52
Cheryl's Birth Certificate Index Number 401018	53
Final Thoughts	54
Photo of Mom and Us as Infants	55
Michelle, Lynn and Cheryl – September 1959- First day of 3rd. Grade	56
Three Photos of Us at Different Ages	57
Mom's Letter to Chery – written in 1992 "Keep looking for *her*."	58
Mom's Short Story, reliving the birthing of her triplet daughters	59/69
<u>**Still Searching**</u> Written on December 14, 1987	
Our Parents Last Photograph Together	70
I Think My Best Friend is Your Identical Twin	71/79
Photos	80/83

Searches

Year	Contact
Dec. 12, 1981	Paulette (sister) worked for Equitable Trust Ins. Co. Paulette said she entered the elevator going up to her work place. She saw a woman that looked exactly like us. I asked her to follow up on this person. The woman's name was Jeanette? She worked there from 1978-1981. It was her last day of work.
March 18, 1886	Unsolved Mysteries – Tim Rogan Supervisor of Productions Without a signed consent form from parents, no go. (spoke 6 times)
Oct. 24, 1986	New York Public Library – I asked them to make a copy of birth Announcements In the newspaper for 1/15/1951.
July 2, 1992	Oprah – phone conversations… many
March 22, 1994	Oprah – Katie Davis & Laura Grant, Producers
June 1994	The Other Side (Parent/Child Connection) – Dr. Will Miller
June 15, 1994	Maury Povich – Federal Express information to Allison
Nov. 23, 1994	Paulette's newspaper picture of a girl playing softball. Looks like us. Stephanie Walls.
Aug. 15, 1995	The Other Side – Sent a tape & script
Aug. 31, 1995	Unsolved Mysteries – Janet Jones, Producer
Sept. 1995	Geraldo's letter
Sept 28, 1995	International Locators – Arlene, Diane
Oct. 25, 1995	Maury Povich – Jan Shalay – Topic: Looking for a twin/ triplet 2/15/96
Nov. 15, 1995	Seekers of the Lost (National Reunion Organization) Katie Katie has *no doubt* that "she" was given up for illegal adoption
Sept. 6, 1995	Find People Fast – called, little could be found
Nov. 24, 1995	Gordon Elliot Show – Sent a tape & script
Dec. 16, 1995	International Locators C/O The Sally Show – Vicki, Producer

Dec. 18, 1995	ALAPC – E-mailed me – try a NY State Adoption Registry such as ALMA *"Our evidence is overwhelming."*
Dec. 27, 1995	Oprah – Margo Green – Told me to call Rat Dog Search Group No reply.
Jan. 2, 1996	Kate Burke C/O Rat Dog Search Group – cannot help us
Feb. 15, 1996	Maury Povich – Without a consent form signed by our parents/ no go May
March 7, 1996	Oprah – Katie Davis – Without a consent form signed by our parents, No/ go.
June 4, 1996	Seekers of the Lost –Sue Smith sent list of females born in NY on 1/15/1951
Dec. 27, 1996	Seekers of the Lost – Sent a tape and script
May 5, 1997	Private Investigator - **Frank L. is hired.**
Dec. 10, 1998	Find People Fast – Sent me results of a search Interesting!
Dec. 30, 1998	Sylvia Brown – Psychic
March 13, 1998	Brian Weiss, MD., P.A. - Seminar
Dec. 18, 2015	International Soundex Reunion Registry – I filled out a form & returned it.
June 2015	Dr. Phil – cannot help us. Too much research to be done
Aug. 2, 2015	Dr. Phil – phone conversation, I followed up, they did not.
Dec. 18, 2015	Genealogist & Private Investigator for N.J. Pamela, No reply.
Sept. 10, 2016	I wrote the first part of the book, Triplet Search
Sept. 18, 2016	I organized my triplet files & created a time line for references.
November 9, 2016	Kristi Hall, Producer for The Dr. Phil Show is interested in hearing more information. We complied with their requests. Now we are waiting to hear from them.
2017	Dr. Phil Show. In 9 months, I wrote three letters. No reply.
Dec. 2017	Published: Lessons Learned and Still Searching
Dec. 22, 2017	Megan Kelly Today Show – Sent her Lessons Learned
Jan. 30, 2018	Megan Kelly Today Show – Sent her Still Searching

Synopsis

- Michelle, Cheryl and friends met HER five or six times at the Farmingdale, L.I. public pool during the summer of 1963.

- Michelle and I saw HER again at Mid-Island Shopping Plaza while we were trying on clothes. <u>This was the first and last time that HER mother saw the three of us together. It was also the last time we ever saw our identical, triplet sister again.</u>

- After many times seeing HER at the pool, our mother finally told us about her pregnancy. Our mom was told that she was having three babies. There was no ultrasound in 1951. Each month, out mother was checked by a different physician, using a stethoscope and finally an x-ray. Her physicians were ready for the birth of three babies. Our mom was told that her babies were going to be born earlier than expected.

- Mary Immaculate Hospital was the welfare hospital for Queens, N.Y. It was managed by priests and nuns. Our mother just turned eighteen years old. Our father was twenty-six and worked for Eastern Airlines.

- On January 15, 1951, our mother gave birth to her first baby girl in the hallway of the hospital. She was rushed into the delivery room where her second baby girl was born.

- When she was pushing her third baby out of the birth canal, the nurses/nuns told her that the doctors were going to anesthetize her in order to repair her vaginal area. <u>She was kept under anesthesia for three days!</u>

- Upon waking up on January 18, 1951, our mother was told that the pushing of the third child was simply afterbirth, not a baby.

Important Facts

- In 1985, I, Cheryl Kaye went to the Ocala, Florida court house to get papers for a pass port. I was told that my documents were not "official." In fact, I was told that I had a "Coverslip Birth Certificate." This meant that I was being tagged to be adopted out to a family, other than my birth parents.

- Michelle Ritson, my twin sister also went to the Orlando court house to obtain a passport. She was told the same thing by the supervisor. The man even asked Michelle if she was adopted!

- Michelle's time of birth was changed from 3:15 to 3:22 on her "Official Certificate of Birth" from Mary Immaculate Hospital.

- Dr. Ryan's signature is different on our birth certificates than on the letter he wrote to our mother on November 20, 1951. (Forgery?)

- Dr. Ryan's signature is also different than the Coverslip Birth Certificates which were to be given to adoptive children. (Forgery?)

- **Cheryl's footprint is on Michelle's Certificate of Birth**

- ***But***

- **Michelle's footprint is *not* on Cheryl's Certificate of Birth from Mary Immaculate Hospital.**

Important documents will follow later in this story.

January 29, 1963

Mom's Verbal Story to Us

Michelle and I were born on January 15, 1951. We were born in Mary Immaculate Hospital located in Jamaica, New York. We were born six weeks earlier than our due date. Michelle weighed 4 lbs.11 oz. I (Cheryl) weighed 5 lbs. 5 oz.

Our mom shared with us this information. "We were told by the nursing staff that babies could not be released from the hospital until they were at least 5 pounds and thriving." "Due to Michelle's low birth weight, you were both kept in hospital incubators for over two weeks. You, Cheryl began to lose weight too. Both of you girls were not being fed properly. We watched you both decline in weight each time we visited, which was every day. It was obvious to us that we had to get you girls out of there."

Mom's story continued. "Due to your grandmother and grandfather's persistence, we decided to get you out of that hospital *that day*. Pappa Redzisz insisted that the nuns produce a birth certificate immediately for both of you.

There was a lot of turmoil in the maternity wing. The priests who were in administration did not want you girls to be released. They said, 'Your girls needed a few more days of incubator care due to their low birth weights. Besides, the certificates will take a few days.' Mom was so emotional when she relived these next details to us but she held it in. "I told the priests, nuns and doctors that I was going to take my babies now! No more waiting. They were mine and I wanted them to come home! You're going to kill them if they stay here.

"Pappa Redzisz went into the nursery and saw you both in a baby incubator. He picked you both up. You were both crying and hungry. He gave one baby to me. We tried to leave the nursery but the nuns tried to stop us. Finally a priest and doctor stood in front of us and said, 'Ok, you can take them. But if they die, that will be on your hands. You will have to sign an order which will hold you responsible if they do." Of course, I said, "They are mine and we are leaving."

Pappa Redzisz told the priest and nuns again, "I want a birth certificate for each of them, now. Within a few minutes, they took both of you girls into a room. In a few minutes, they returned you to us along with birth certificates and we drove home.

Looking back

Looking back, now we understand why the doctor, nuns and priests did not want to release Michelle and me. We were going to be adopted out, just like *her*.

In Search of Our Triplet Sister - 1963

During the summer of 1963, when my sister, Michelle and I turned twelve years old, we lived in Farmingdale, Long Island, New York. As young girls, Michelle and I never knew that we had a triplet sister, until the three of us met by accident several times, at a public swimming pool located in our town.

Michelle and I would walk to the public pool with our friends. We visited there almost every weekend during the summer. The walk took us about 30 minutes. The entire route was almost all sidewalks. It was a fun walk. We loved being a part of this town. We all felt safe walking to and from our weekly destination.

We always passed Pete's Deli on the corner of Main Street. Sometimes we would buy a hard roll with butter and a Coke. This kept us full for a few hours. Then, on the way home we always stopped at Alfonzo's Pizza Parlor and treated ourselves to a slice of delicious pizza and an egg-cream soda.

Our friends were Lynn, Susan, and Alper. Michelle and I spent many years together with Susan and Lynn playing outside. We were close friends and the same age. Alper was about eight and spoke very little English. He and his family just moved from Turkey to the United States. When we arrived at the pool, we entered through a cyclone fence gate. Concrete surrounded the entire fenced in area. The cost was twenty five cents per person. The pool was not that large, however it had a deeper area that was roped off for kids who wanted to practice their dives off the board. The pool and sitting areas were always full of busy children and teenagers. It was the "in place" to meet friends!

The five of us carried towels. We spread them out beside the fence so we could save our spot. All four of us girls put our colorful bathing caps on and walked into the water to play leap frog with Alper. Speaking little English, he made the funniest facial looks, hand gestures and sounds when playing with us. We all knew what he was trying to say. Leap Frog was not that complicated a game.

The first time the three of us "identical sisters" noticed each other is a time Michelle and I will never forget. We had no prior knowledge of us having a triplet sister. This was a real shock to all of us. I can still remember seeing *her* for the first time as if it was yesterday.

****

Leap Frog

Playing Leap Frog in the water was a fun and mindless game. It was like playing tag. Instead of tagging the person who was *it*, they would have to dunk the other person's head under water and then get away fast.

It was Alper's turn to be *it*. He jumped around while making lots of waves and splashing everyone as he looked in all directions for one of us to dunk. With lots of vigor, I saw Alper jump on top of a girl's shoulders. He was trying to dunk her head under the water. She kept swatting Alper, trying to push him away from her. I'm sure she thought this boy was crazy!

Alper must have thought that she was Michelle or me, Cheryl. But, all four of us girls were standing about ten feet away from Alper. We all watched him wrestle with the other girl, but who was she?

Michelle and I were standing side by side in the pool along with girlfriends, Lynn and Susan. I remember thinking, "If my sister is right next to me, then who is he dunking? I could have sworn that Alper was dunking Michelle. Michelle thought the same about me!

Almost immediately, Alper saw all four of us standing together staring at him. When he saw Michelle and me standing shoulder to shoulder with our friends, he leaped off of *her* shoulders and screamed, "YIKES!" Then it happened, *she* turned around to look at us too.

Lynn, Susan, Alper, Michelle and I gathered closely, still in the water and began endless chattering questions about who this identical girl was. This was absolutely nuts! We couldn't believe our eyes. Who the heck was she? Where did she come from? Why did she look so much like Michelle and me? Did she go to school here too?

Since Michelle and I were painfully shy, we urged our friends to go over to *her* and ask questions while we were all still in the moment. But she slowly took off her bathing cap and got out of the pool, all the while never looking up at any of us.

With her cap off her head, she looked even more like us. For the rest of the day, we all continued to stare at one another. Alper tried to get her to come over to our towel by being silly and playful but she continued to sit on her towel alone. We all made lots of eye contact that day. Lots of sneaking a peek at each other, trying not to be too noticeable.

We all had the same blue eyes, sandy blonde hair and were the same height. I couldn't believe that she even had the same nose as us. Looking at her was like looking at a reflection of myself. I am sure she was just as confused as we were. She made no effort to come over to us either. We were all shy.

Something unusual happened to Michelle and me that day. Talking about *her* to each other, we both felt as if we had known this identical girl forever. We were so comfortable just looking at her, watching her and seeing how she ate her snack or drank her drink. There was nothing unfamiliar about her mannerisms. She even acted like us!

About four in the afternoon, a car pulled up in front of the gate and a woman got out of the car and waved to *her* in the pool area. Michelle and I made an observation about the woman who always picked *her* up. Our mother was only thirty years old and very young looking. This woman looked to be much older, possible a young grandmother.

Before getting into the car *she* turned around to stare at us one more time. Michelle and I watched as the car drove off. We expected to see the identical girl again next weekend.

We saw her about five more times that summer. Gosh, we love seeing her. We couldn't wait to make eye contact with each other. Michelle and I agreed that we felt complete now. I believe that to be so, even to this day. If we had it to do over again, with our maturity, I am SURE that we would have tried to make friends with her. She was always alone. At least Michelle and I had each other.

****

Questions, Questions, Questions

Upon returning home, Michelle and I told our mother about seeing a girl who looked exactly like us at the pool. Our mom was not too interested in what we had to say and simply said, "Oh you girls have such common Polish faces. There are lots of pretty Polish girls out there!" Of course, Michelle and I believed her and dropped the conversation with our mom, but not with each other.

In the days that followed, Michelle and I were giddy with excitement about seeing this identical looking girl again. As usual, Saturday morning came. This time, only Michelle and I went to the pool together, without our friends. We wanted to be at the pool before ten that morning. This way, we could watch everyone who came to the pool through the entry gate.

The same older woman dropped her off at the pool shortly after ten am. She was sitting on the other side of the pool, all by herself again. She didn't have any friends and seemed to know no one. Michelle and I moved our towels down by her side of the pool to be closer to her. We three shared lots of shy smiles that day, but no conversations. It was a long day, waiting for one of us to make the brave move and say, "Hi." But, that never happened.

We saw each other a few more times again that summer. I could tell that she looked forward to our pool visits too. It was very comfortable seeing her and being near her. We were so young and shy. We never expected those wonderful encounters to end.

Naïve and unsuspecting, we never thought for one moment that being a twin was unique. I always had my close friend close by, so did Michelle. Therefore, wanting to meet other friends was very limited. Having each other, we were complete. However, when the three of us were close to each other, I could tell that *we all shared the same, internal and emotional feelings.* There was no need to talk.

Michelle and I walked home very slowly from the pool that day. We tossed a lot of thoughts around with each other. Of course, we both saw *her* mom pick *her* up again. This time, I looked very carefully at her mom. I didn't recognize her. We both decided that we would talk to our mom again when we got home. Our want and need to know *her* was becoming very important to us. How I wish I knew her name. It wouldn't make her any less real though. We had to talk to our mom again.

We walked into the house and saw our mom sitting at the kitchen table, reading a book. She loved to read. I was the courageous twin so I started the conversation by saying, "We saw her again, Mom." I put a lot of emphasis on the word, "her." She listened to us with genuine interest this time.

Finally, our mom asked us both to sit down with her at the small table in the kitchen. For the first time ever, our mom opened up to us that day as if we were young adults, not kids. Until now, I always felt unimportant. Today changed everything. Mom's story was mixed with excitement, sadness and confusion. At twelve, this was lot of information to take in. It still is, to this day.

This is what she said to us.

"I was seventeen and your father was twenty-six when we were married. He was a Korean War Veteran with severe emotional problems. *PTSD, was not recognized at that time.* Several months after he came home from Burma, he found a job working for Eastern Airlines as a mechanic and a plane cleaner. Your dad said he loved me very much. I wasn't in love. At seventeen, what the heck did I know?" She bowed her head and wiped tears away from her eyes, but continued.

"On a Sunday afternoon, after the mid-day meal with his family in Jamaica, your dad gave me an engagement ring. I was totally surprised and shocked. I was not expecting a ring at all. I didn't know what to expect from a marriage but it felt good to be a part of a vibrant family. Besides, it was better than living at home with my parents, so I accepted. Shortly afterwards, we were married in a beautiful Catholic church. My mother even made my wedding gown. It was beautiful."

Michelle and I were hearing this for the first time. "We lived on the second floor of his mother's row house, in Jamaica, N.Y. This was not the best part of town to live in. I used to babysit for the family who lived across the street on Jamaica Avenue almost every day. I was always afraid to leave the house, but I felt safe there. Three months later, your dad and I found out I was pregnant."

Mom looked at us and said, "I didn't realize how poor we were until I was told that we had to go to a welfare hospital for my prenatal visits. Gosh, we were so stupid. We didn't know that your dad had very good medical insurance. Knowing this would have help us so much. Hindsight is a wonderful thing!"

She continued, "By the third month of my pregnancy, I was told that I was carrying triplets! Three distinct heartbeats were heard. I remember several doctors and nurses came into the room to check this out for themselves. Triplet births were not the usual thing for any hospital. Ultrasound was not invented yet, so a stethoscope was the only way to check on my babies. Everyone seemed to be very excited, even me." Mom looked so sad.

"For the next four and a half months of my pregnancy, I went to Mary Immaculate Hospital for my prenatal check-ups. Sometimes I took a train. Other times, my parents would come and pick me up and take me there. Mary Immaculate Hospital was the welfare hospital in Queens, N.Y. During each visit, I saw a different doctor. My check-ups always seemed important to all who came to see me. The rooms were dark, dingy and very outdated.

Michelle and I hung onto every word. This was all new to us.

"The nurses were Catholic nuns. They wore their starched, white caps along with a simple, white robe. Some nuns wore their long, black robes and full habit. Priests walked the halls and worked in administration. I was always afraid of these stoic men. I never trusted any of them.

In my fifth month of pregnancy, I was asked to come back for my prenatal visits every two weeks. There was no doubt that three heartbeats were heard. Each beat was distinct and clear. I was told that my babies were strong and doing very well. There were always different doctors, nurses and priests coming into my room to hear the heartbeats. By now, I felt special and very protective over my babies that I was carrying."

Mom looked at us and we noticed how proud she looked.

"Towards the end of my pregnancy, an x-ray was taken due to the possibility of renal failure. The pregnancy was very rough on me. I was huge and very uncomfortable but healthy. The x-rays showed a third shadow hiding behind two of the babies. We were all elated that I was going to deliver triplets!

The day came when my water broke, six weeks earlier than my due date. I was told that this was not unusual because multiple births are usually born early. My parents drove your dad and me to the hospital. It all happened so fast."

Michelle and I didn't move, for fear that our mother would stop talking. It seemed so difficult for her to remember these moments. She seemed to choose her words very carefully.

"One baby girl was born in the hallway of the hospital. There was a rush of people all around me as they wheeled me into a delivery room. My second baby girl was born a few minutes later in the room. I was totally awake for both births."

Now our mom was getting emotional and found it difficult to contain her anger for what she was about to tell us.

"There were a lot of people buzzing around in my delivery room. I remember the nun in charge, briskly left my delivery room, after the two births. She went to the waiting room to tell your dad and my parents that we had two girls, and there was another baby on the way! I was told later on, by my parents, that your dad's response was, "What the hell am I going to do with three girls? I don't make enough money as it is to take care of Janie and myself. He was totally distraught and angry. He wanted a son."

Michelle and I said, "*Oh*" at the same time. We waited to hear more of her story.

"One of the doctors told me that I was going to be anesthetized because of complications. He told me that there would be some sutures due to some tearing of my birth canal. I was kept unconscious for three, full days." ***How could that happen? I thought.***

"When the doctors-priests finally woke me up, I remember asking for my three babies. A nurse-nun told me that I had two, healthy, beautiful, little girls. But I remembered pushing another baby out. I heard a distinct cry, then I was put to sleep. The nun told me again that there was no third baby. She said it was the afterbirth, the sac that the two girls were born in.

But in November, I wrote Dr. Ryan a letter and asked if you girls were identical or fraternal. He told me that he could not be sure because there were two sacs."

Our mother continued, "What the heck was I going to do? It was me against the priest and nuns. They treated me as if I was a stupid, young girl… and I was. They kept me asleep for three days! Why? What did they do with my third baby? I heard a baby cry. She was mine and they took her. They took her!"

Mom broke down in tears. We have never seen our mother cry like this. She was actually grief stricken. Once our mom calmed down, she asked us never to mention this to our father. She said that she tried to talk this over with him once, when we were first brought home from the hospital. Mom said our dad went into a rage.

She never mentioned the third baby again, *until today… twelve years later.*

****

Mid-Island Shopping Plaza We Meet For the Last Time… 1963

In private our mother told us, "The next time you see *her*, get a license plate number. Try to get a description of the car too." We had a neighbor who was a sergeant in the police department. She planned on giving Mr. Vernon Boyd the plate number in hopes that he could trace the name of the vehicle's owner. Of course, he said he would be glad to help.

Shortly before the end of summer, the public pool closed. Michelle and I thought we would never see *her* again. We talked about her a lot and wondered what she liked to do outside of the pool. Did she like horses like me or did she like to draw and design dresses like Michelle? Did she live close by or was she visiting for the summer? Why was she taken away from our family? We had too many questions and not enough answers.

A few weeks passed and the two of us went into town. We decided to look at the back-to-school clothes in Mid-Island. It was a small but modern department store in Farmingdale. I loved that old store. It had oak floors which creaked each time we took a few steps.

It didn't take long for each of us to pick out a few outfits. There were three dressing rooms with doors located in the middle of the store. Each room held enough space for one person. We each had our own dressing room. In order to see yourself, you had to come out of the room. The mirror was on the back of the door.

Michelle came out of her dressing room and stood in front of the full-length mirror. She had on a new Ship-N-Shore, no-iron blouse, with a tweed skirt and matching jacket. This was the new trend for the fall.

I was still trying on my outfit when I heard Michelle say, "Well, what do you think of this?" Then I heard Michelle say in a louder voice, "Answer me, Stupid!" The next thing I heard was a slap. Not knowing who my sister just slapped, I came out of my room still buttoning up my jacket and froze.

Here was our *third sister* again, standing less than two feet away from Michelle and me. Neither one of us moved. The three of us just stood there in silence looking each other over. Michelle whispered, "It's *her*." I remember smiling and letting out a happy laugh while saying, "We never thought that we would see you again." It was a wonderful moment.

She broke up the situation and slowly walked away from us while strolling through the clothing isles. She continued to exchange inquisitive glances at us. She joined up with the familiar, older woman who was in the check-out-line. Quietly they shared a few brief words. The woman looked at Michelle and me for a few seconds. Without any delay, the woman set her intended purchase items down and took *her* by the elbow. They both exited the door without looking back.

At that moment, we remembered what our mother told us to do if we ever saw *her* again. "Get a license plate number and car description." We both said, "Get dressed!" at the same time. We wanted to run after them but Michelle and I had to change back into our street clothes first. As quickly as we could, we changed.

I ran out the front door and searched the parking spaces that lined Main Street. No luck. Michelle walked as fast as she could towards the back of the store. She pushed the glass doors open and began to look for the car in the parking lots. No luck either.

We never saw her again.

****

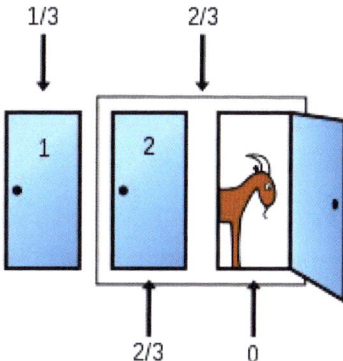

Time Lapsed into Years

Lots of things happened since we were in grade school. We graduated from Farmingdale High School on Long Island, N.Y. in 1968 instead of 1969, a year earlier than all of our friends. We skipped our senior year. We were seventeen. Why wait? We had all of our credits. We were ready to enter the workplace and become independent.

We bought a 1962 Chevy Nova together, worked during the day and went to Nassau Community College at night. "Real life" was so much more rewarding than the high school days. No regrets for skipping the drama.

Yes, we let years lapse until Michelle and I were once more beginning to search for our triplet sister. We didn't begin searching again until 1981.

We both left the state of New York in 1970. Michelle moved to sunny Florida, where she perused a nursing and eventually a real estate career. She still resides there today. My husband and I lived in Charleston, South Carolina for three years while he served his time as an Officer on a Mine Sweeper for the Navy. We relocated to Maryland in 1973. I completed my BS. Degree at the University of Maryland in 1975 and he continued to work for the U.S. Navy as an engineer.

In 1980, I moved to Hernando, Florida to be closer to my twin sister, Michelle. I call her, Mickey. I remarried in 1985. My new husband was also an identical twin. Sure, we moved several times for the sake of our husband's jobs, but we never stopped looking for our third twin!

****

In the *Searches* section of this book, I listed all of the years that I contacted television shows, producers and psychics. We haven't found *her*, yet. It was not for a lack of trying though.

****

The story begins again…

Our Easter Vacation in 1984 - Clearwater, Florida

What better way to spend an Easter vacation away from teaching in Inverness, Florida than to head across the state to Clearwater. Michelle and I packed up our recreational vehicle with enough food to last a week. The four kids were ready for our first "road trip" together. Michelle had two young daughters, ages five and seven. My daughter was also five and my son was eight.

I wanted to attend my first Florida Easter sunrise, church service there. We were all excited to explore the sights and sounds of this beautiful area.

I recently purchased a beautiful Minolta camera and several lenses from a department store in Ocala, Florida. It *was* a beautiful camera. I say "was" because I put it down on the bumper of the rv just long enough to tie my daughter's laces on her sneakers. I turned around to pick it up, and it was gone. Someone stole my new camera. After lots of searching, we gave up. As soon as we returned home to Hernando, I reported my expensive camera as stolen to the local police department in Inverness. I filled out all the necessary paperwork and provided receipts to prove it was a Minolta. Their detective gave me the phone number and name of a contact detective in Clearwater. Of course, I made contact with their supervisor regarding my stolen camera. Almost a year passed without any luck for finding my camera bag and accessories.

****

In October of 1985, I received a phone call from an Officer Al Hogue. Al and I dated for about a year until I met and married Ray Kaye in May 1985. Ray and I lived in Ocala after we were married. Al was now a detective and forensic photographer who worked in Inverness.

I asked Al why he was calling me. He knew that I married Ray. I wasn't comfortable having him call me.

Well, to my surprise he said, "I have information about your missing camera that you lost in Clearwater."

I was thrilled to hear the great news. Maybe I would be able to get the camera back. I took so many wonderful photos of the kids at our sunrise service. *It was wishful thinking.*

"Can you meet me somewhere so I can show you some photos that were in the camera when it was found?

Eagerly I said, "Sure. Let's meet at Bennigan's Restaurant in thirty minutes." I was so interested in finding out why he had my camera after all these months. Most of all, I wanted my photos of the kids.

Al said, "Ok. See you then." We hung up.

I entered the restaurant and immediately saw Al sitting at a table waiting for me to join him. I gave him a gentle hug and we exchanged small talk for a little while about our families and jobs. I noticed that Al was acting very cool and aloof towards me. I accepted his mannerisms as normal, since I married someone else and not him.

He took an envelope of photos out of his jacket and placed it on the table. As quickly as I could, I rummaged through the photographs. I lost my breath. I was confused. I stared at the photos and asked him, "Who are these people? Where did you get these photos?"

All he did was look at me with that typical, police office look of suspicion written all over his face. The once friendly Al was now interrogating *me* about the photos. But why? I was the one who had questions.

Al knew that I had been searching for my identical, triplet sister for many years. He shoved another black and white photo across the table for me to see. I was shocked beyond belief. "Who is this woman? Who are the twins that she is holding in each hand?"

Al had a cold look on his face. He said, "You tell me."

"What are you talking about? Where did you find these photos?" I asked him again.

"Isn't this you, Chery? Who are these twin girls?" He asked me.

"Al, look at me. This must be my triplet sister. It's not me. You know my kids are Matt and Amy, not five year old identical twin girls!"

Clearly, Al did not believe me. He really thought that the woman in the photos was me. He was not going to give up either. He kept asking me the same questions in different ways; as if he was trying to trick me into telling him, "Yes, it was me." *But it was not!*

Now, I was upset, anxious and angry that Al was actually convinced that I was the woman in the photos.

I looked at Al and said, "Ok Al. Turn off the dramatics and be honest with me. I have seen your cop attitude before and you are really ticking me off. Talk to me now, or I am leaving. As soon as I said these words, he softened up his facial features and relaxed. I think he finally believed me. *I was not the woman in the photos!*

****

I looked directly into his eyes and raised my voice ever so slightly and said, "Tell me."

"Ok. I will tell you what I know."

Al took out another piece of paper from his inside pocket and read it to me.

"The rented room of a man Clearwater Police shot and killed on September 12th, contained the property of at least twelve Citrus County residents. Among the stolen property was a computer from attorney Jeanette Haag, property belonging to the King B. Construction Company in Lecanto, property belonging to Lewis Seward and Eugene Morries of Homosassa, property belonging to renters of storage units in Homosassa and other goods belonging to several others in the county."

Al continued, "Inside the rented room was a camera. I immediately thought of you, although it wasn't a Minolta, like yours. I developed the film and couldn't believe my eyes. I could have sworn these photos were of you, Chery. That's why I am here. I wanted you to see the photos for yourself."

I continued to read the entire newspaper article and shook my head. There was too much information in the article for me to digest. We spent over an hour together talking about who this woman and her twin girls were in the photos. Could this be my triplet sister?

He told me that he would get back to the office to share his "findings" with his supervisor.

Officer Al Hogue was finally convinced. The woman with the twin girls in the photos was not me.

****

We never did find out who she was. I contacted the Clearwater Police Department. I spoke to Detective Jim Gravely many times. He understood that I was searching for our triplet sister. This woman might be her.

I asked Detective Gravely if he would put one of her photos in the Clearwater newspaper. Maybe someone would recognize her. It's all I could hope for. It might help his case and mine. He said, "Of course."

Several days later, he sent me a copy of the article and photograph, entitled SEARCH. I have each article listed separately.

- Burglar killed by Clearwater police suspected in a dozen Citrus burglaries.
- SEARCH

October 1985
Inverness Newspaper

Burglar killed by Clearwater police suspected in a dozen Citrus burglaries

By STEVE ARTHUR
Staff Writer

The rented room of a man Clearwater Police shot and killed on Sept. 12 contained the property of at least 12 Citrus County residents, according to a Sheriff's department spokesman.

Among the stolen property was a computer belonging to attorney Jeannette Haag, property belonging to the King B Construction Company in Lecanto, property belonging to Lewis Seward and Eugene Morries of Homosassa, property belonging to renters of storage units in Homosassa, and goods belonging to several others in the county.

According to Sheriff's investigator Les Cross, a 33-year-old man whose real name is believed to have been Charles Lockwood, lived and worked in Citrus County during most of July.

Cross said Lockwood, who was known by a number of aliases, including William A. Moore and Eugene Lockwood, worked for an area mobile home dealer while living in Citrus County. Cross said Lockwood held a Homosassa Springs post office box during that time.

Lockwood moved from Citrus County late in July, Cross said, but the Orange County Sheriff's Department was looking for him with warrants charging Lockwood with grand theft and burglary. Lockwood was believed to have stolen a van from an Orange County impoundment lot before leaving that county.

The Citrus investigator said investigators from Orange County had reason to believe Lockwood had moved to Clearwater. Police there were notified and on Sept. 24 went to a Clearwater firm where Lockwood was believed to be employed.

Please see burglaries, back page

Burglaries

Continued from page one

While Clearwater Police were talking to his boss, Lockwood ran into a wooded area to escape arrest. While police were called to search the area into which he fled, other officers were put on stakeout at his rented room.

That evening, according to Cross, Lockwood was seen approaching his room and when officers called for him to surrender, he fired at the police. They returned fire and he was wounded, but ran.

As officers moved on him, Cross said Lockwood first held a pistol to his head, as if to kill himself, then pointed his pistol at police, who killed him.

The small one-bedroom Clearwater house Lockwood had rented was filled with stolen property, Cross said, and among the property, many of the items found were determined to be from Citrus County.

Property owners who had recorded serial numbers of their property before it was stolen had turned that information over to Citrus Investigators, who entered the information into the Florida Crime Information Center's computer, which is also hooked into the National Crime Information Center's computer.

Cross said he and investigator Woody Lucius have already identified and turned property over to their rightful owners, and plan to return more in the near future.

They are also seeking the owners of other property, some of which hasn't yet been reported stolen. Cross said they found a driver's license belonging to Linda Lehnertz and a Sears Credit Card still in its envelope, belonging to Audrey Cutler.

1985 - October Clearwater Newspaper

Search

Citrus County Sheriff's investigators are searching for the woman in the photo in the belief that she may be one of the Citrus burglary victims robbed by a man Clearwater Police shot and killed on Sept. 12. The man, identified as Charles Lockwood, is believed to have worked here in July and lived under a series of aliases. A number of items stolen from Citrus residents has already been recovered. The sheriff's investigators ask that persons able to identify the woman call investigator Les Cross at 726-4488.

Department of Police

City of Clearwater

644 Pierce Street
Clearwater, Florida
33516
813/462/6000

24 OCT. 1985

CHERYL KAYE
5147 S.E. 14TH PL.
OCALA, FL. 32671

DEAR CHERYL,

    I HAVE ENCLOSED ALL OF THE NEGATIVES THAT I HAVE. I HAVE ALSO SENT SOME OF THE PRINTS THAT I HAD. I WILL HOLD ONTO THE REMAINING PRINTS JUST IN CASE SOMETHING SHOULD ARISE. IT APPEARS THAT YOU HAVE A CHORE CUT OUT FOR YOU AND I WISH YOU A LOT OF LUCK. I'LL CONTACT YOU SHOULD ANYTHING COME FROM THE PHOTO BEING IN THE NEWSPAPER. DON'T HESITATE TO CALL IF I CAN BE OF SOME HELP.

SINCERELY,

Det Jim Gravely

DET. JIM GRAVELY

What is a Coverslip Birth Certificate?
Ocala, Florida

In 1985, I went to the court house in Ocala, Fl. I wanted to pick up paperwork to obtain a passport. My new husband, Ray Kaye wanted to take me to Europe and I needed one.

I was told to bring in a birth certificate and driver's license. When my name was called, I took out the document which I thought was my birth certificate. I handed it to the woman behind the desk along with my driver's license.

She looked at my certificate and handed it back to me while saying, "This is not an official birth certificate. It is a coverslip document." I asked what a coverslip document was. She said, "Coverslips are attached to children that are slotted for adoption. Are you adopted?" I answered curtly, "No, I am not adopted."

She softened her tone when she saw the confused look on my face and said, "Coverslips are put in the files of children who are to be adopted out. If you are sure that you were *not* adopted, then you can get an official certificate from The Department of Health/The Bureau of Vital Records in New York." I said, "OK. Thank you" and left.

When I got home, I called my sister, Michelle and told her that we both were slotted out to be adopted! I asked her if she had her certificate and asked her what it looked like. She told me that it was black with white lettering. "Yup, we were next in line to be adopted."

The next call I made was to our mother. I told her what the Ocala office told me and she said," Holy ****." Then I said, "Mom, it looks like we were going to be adopted too." She said, "Oh my God! Now I know why the priests, nuns and doctors wanted to keep you girls for a few more days at the hospital. They would have told me you were losing weight and died, clearing the way for you both to be given away to someone else."

Mom sobbed. "Papa Redzisz was right all along. He told me not to trust the welfare hospital and to get you girls home immediately. We wouldn't leave that day without you. Now I know why everyone wanted us to go home and come back tomorrow. Mary Immaculate Hospital had plans of their own."

Cheryl's Coverslip Birth Certificate

A coverslip birth certificate is a special document.

Coverslips are attached to a child's file if the child is to be placed up for adoption.

Dr. Ryan's signature is <u>not</u> the same signature as seen on

1. Dr. Ryan's letter to our mom on Nov. 20, 1951 *OR*
2. Mary Immaculate Hospital's Certificate of Birth.

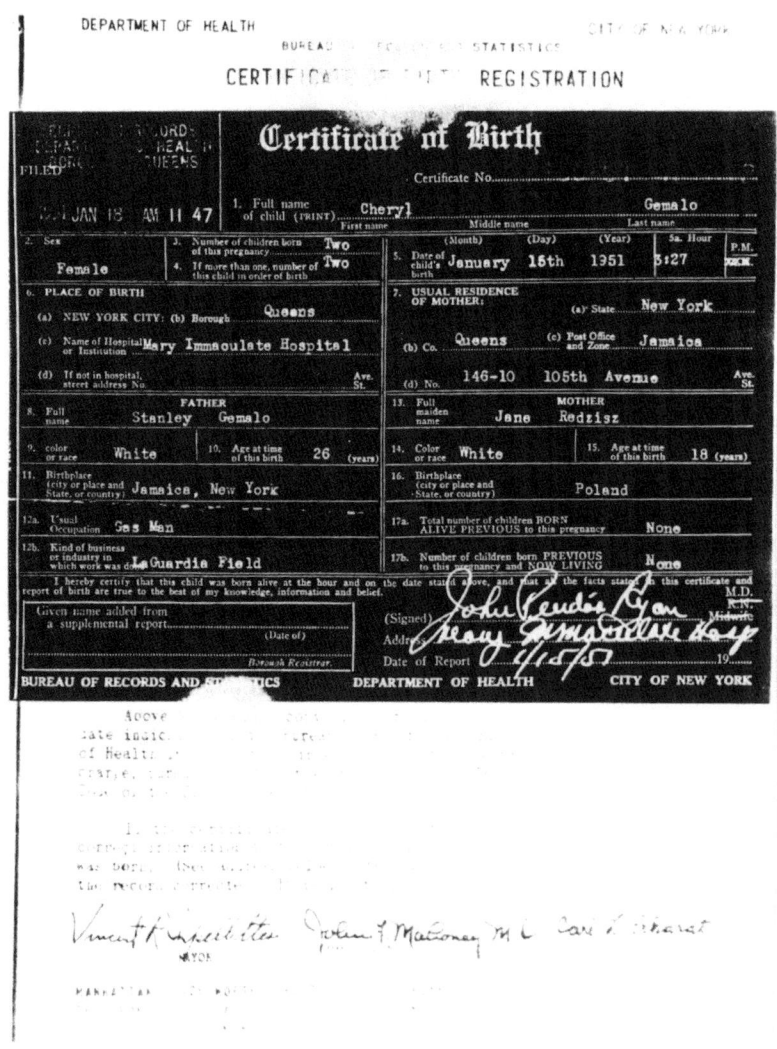

November 20, 1951

Dr. John P. Ryan's Letter to Our Mom, Jane Gemalo

Our mother was very interested in knowing if Michelle and I (Cheryl) were either identical or fraternal twins. We were 10 months old. She knew that she gave birth to triplets. She also knew that she couldn't talk this over with our father, Stanley Gemalo; so, she wrote a letter to her pediatrician-doctor at Mary Immaculate Hospital. We still have the original letter and envelope that Dr. Ryan sent to our mother. A copy of the doctor's letter is on the next page.

Here is Dr. Ryan's reply to our mom.

Mary Immaculate Hospital
152-11 89th. Avenue
Jamaica 2, N.Y.

November 20, 1951

Mrs. Jane Gemalo
412 Farmingdale Road
West Babylon, New York

Dear Mrs. Gemalo:

I cannot say that your twins are identical. At the time of delivery, one placenta with two cords and two sacs was found. With these findings, I would infer that the twins are identical. But, on the basis that two placentas can become fused as one, I am still uncertain as to whether they are identical or not identical. This is all the evidence I have.

Sincerely yours,
MARY IMMACULATE HOSPITAL

JCR/CH.   By: John P. Ryan M.D.

Dr. Ryan's signature was signed in cursive using his entire name, John P. Ryan M.D. The signature of this doctor is the same one that is on our "coverslip" birth certificate. It is a confirmation that the doctor's signature on the Mary Immaculate Hospital certificate is not Dr. Ryan's signature.

Please compare these signatures carefully. The original is on the next page.

MARY IMMACULATE HOSPITAL
152-11 89TH AVENUE
JAMAICA 2, N. Y.

November 20, 1951.

Mrs. Jane Gemalo
412 Farmingdale Road
West Babylon, New York.

Dear Mrs. Gemalo:

I cannot say that your twins are identical. At the time of delivery, one placenta with two cords and two sacs was found. With these findings, I would infer that the twins are identical. But, on the basis that two placentas can become fused as one, I am still uncertain as to whether they are identical or not identical. This is all the evidence I have.

Sincerely yours,
MARY IMMACULATE HOSPITAL.

JOR/CH.

By *John P. Ryan M.D.*

November 20, 1951

Dr. Ryan's letter to our mother

The physician's signature appears to be the same as our Coverslip birth certificates.

This confirms that the signature on the "Official" Certificate of Birth is **not** Dr. Ryan's.

Cheryl's Official Ceritificate of Birth from M.I.H.

This document has an official seal.

Dr. Ryan, the attending physician's signature is different than on his letter to our mom on November, 2, 1951.

Mary Immaculate Hospital

In Charge of the Sisters of St. Dominic

JAMAICA, NEW YORK

Certificate of Birth

This Certifies that _Cheryl Gemalo "B"_ was born to _Jane and Stanley Gemalo_ in this Hospital at _3:27_ p.m. the _fifteenth_ day of _January_ A.D. 19_51_.

In Witness Whereof the said Hospital has caused this Certificate to be signed by its duly authorized officers and its Official Seal to be hereunto affixed.

Dr. Ryan, Attending Physician

Sister Ursula Marie, O.P., Superintendent

Michelle's "Official Certificate of Birth" from M.I.H.

The time of birth has been altered. It appears to be 3:15. It was changed to read 3:22.

This document has an official hospital seal.

Dr. Ryan, the attending physician's signature is different than his letter to our mom on Nov. 20, 1951.

Dr. Ryan's signature is also different than the Coverslip Birth Certificate

Mary Immaculate Hospital

In Charge of the Sisters of St. Dominic

JAMAICA, NEW YORK

Certificate of Birth

This Certifies that _Michelle Gencalo_ was born to _Jane and Stanley Gencalo_ in this Hospital at _3:22_ P.m. the _Fifteenth_ day of _January_ A.D. 19_57_ In Witness Whereof the said Hospital has caused this Certificate to be signed by its duly authorized officers and its Official Seal to be hereunto affixed.

Dr. Ryan
Attending Physician

Sister Ursula Marie O.P.

NO. _____
3/22 19 8 x
RECEIVED FROM Cheryl Kay
Five ——————————————— DOLLARS
Foot Prints

Account Total $ _____
Amount Paid $ 5.00
Balance Due $ _____

"THE EFFICIENCY LINE" AN AMPAD PRODUCT

CAPT JONES #904
SGT FREEMAN #964
Newton Co. S.O.
784-2105

IN SHORT: Cheryl's foot print is on Michelle's birth certificate but Michelle's foot print is not on Cheryl's birth certificate.

From 1990 to 2000, I taught at Sharp Middle School which is located in Covington, Georgia, S. E. of Atlanta. In The Heat of the Night was being filmed at our school. The entire cast and crew showed up after school and on weekends. A few scenes were filmed in my classroom, which was really a garage. I taught Vocational Agriculture and Plant Science so a cement floor was perfect when watering plants.

A policeman introduced himself to me one afternoon as he entered my classroom. He started to remove all of the desks and plants. He told me, "Within the next few hours, your room will be converted into a ball room." I was surprised but I loved being part of a television program.

We got to talking and I told him about my search for my triplet sister. He shared with me several stories that were going around Covington about missing family members. I laughed and said, "No it's not like that. She has not been abducted. She was adopted at birth." He told me to go to the Sheriff's Office and ask for Sargent Freeman. Maybe he could help me. "Bring your birth certificate too."

So, on March 22, 1994 I found my way over to the police department. I walked up to the window inside the corridor and asked for Sargent Freeman. I was asked to sit down and wait for him, so I did.

Sargent Freeman asked me why I wanted to have my feet *inked?* I told him that my birth certificate did not have hand prints on it. It only had foot prints and we wanted to compare our actual footprints to the prints on the certificates. "Oh," he said. "Come on in." He buzzed the locked door open and I walked into an office.

He told me to take off my socks, so I did. He carefully washed off my left foot first. Then he dried it. We waited a few moments and then he rolled black ink over the bottom of my foot. He took out a piece of white paper and said, "Now step on this carefully." He did the same to my right foot. I told him that I would be back in a few weeks so he could roll my twin sister's feet too. He said, "Fine, see you then."

Three weeks later, I brought Michelle into the police department. She lived in Windermere, Florida. We planned to spend a fun weekend together. Once again, I asked to see Sargent Freeman. He made a few jokes about how identical we looked. At the same time, he buzzed us into his office. He got out his supplies and told Michelle to carefully wash off her feet. Once they were dry, Sargent Freeman rolled black ink over her left foot, then her right foot. Her prints were clear and bold.

The Sargent asked me to bring our birth certificates and my foot prints when we came, so I did. He carefully examined and compared our foot prints against the birth certificate prints. After a few minutes he told us something that shocked us all.

Sargent Freeman said, "Hmmm, Cheryl's foot print is on Michelle's birth certificate **but** Michelle's foot print is **not** on Cheryl's birth certificate."

I immediately said, "Oh My Gosh, then whose footprint is on my certificate? Could it be Ellen's?" He looked at the both of us and simply shook his head and said, "Stranger things have happened. Good luck with your search girls. Call me if you need me." We thanked him and left the police department.

Could we really have something now?

LEFT FOOT

This is to Certify that these are my Foot Print

2/22/94 X Cheryl Kaye

Prints Taken By

2/22/94 Sgt. K. W. Jr #964

NEWTON COUNTY DETENTION FACILITY
1154 STAL...
COVINGTON, ...
(404) 784-2103

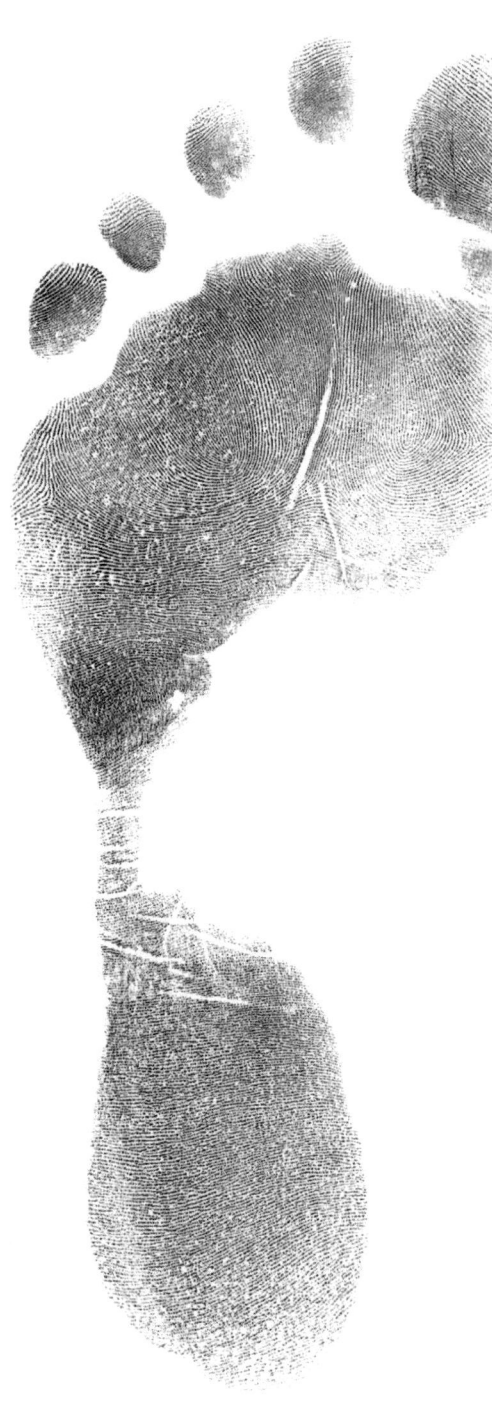

Right Foot - Cheryl Kaye

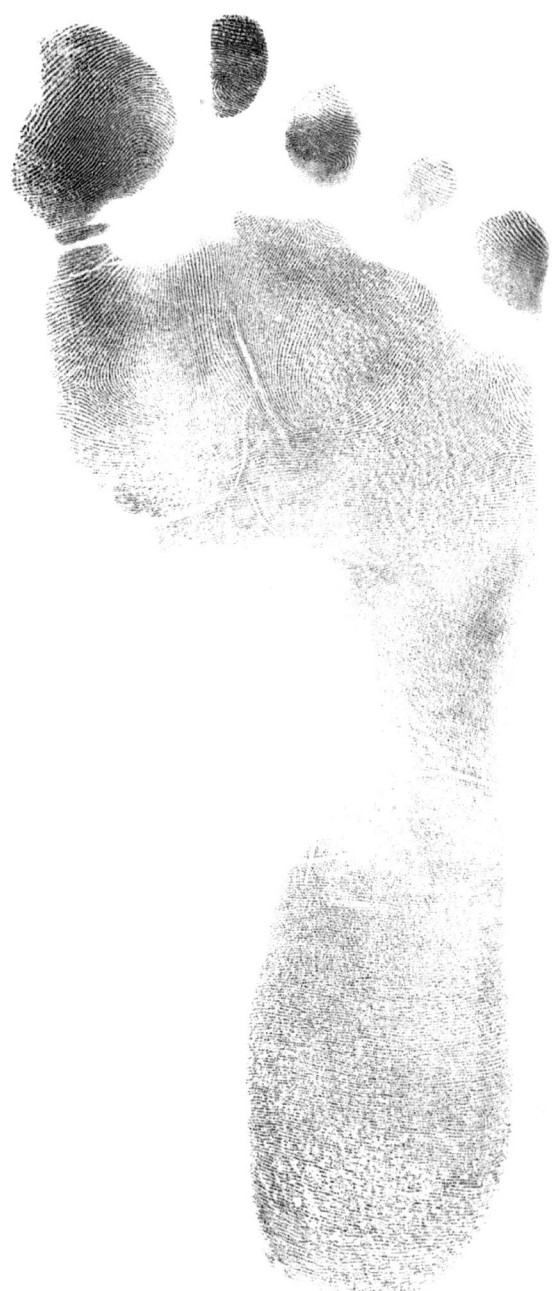

NEWTON COUNTY DETENTION FACILITY
1154 STALLINGS ST.
COVINGTON, GA 30209
(404) 784-2103

michelle

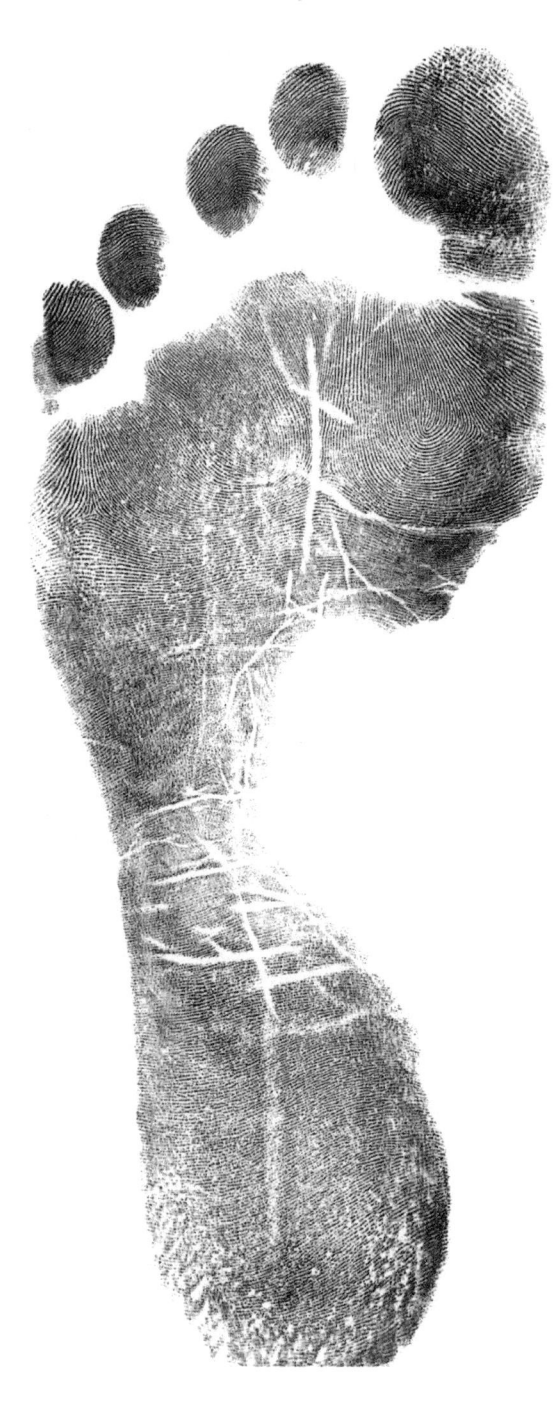

NEWTON COUNTY DETENTION FACILITY
1154 STALLINGS ST.
COVINGTON, GA 30209
(404) 784-2103

michelle

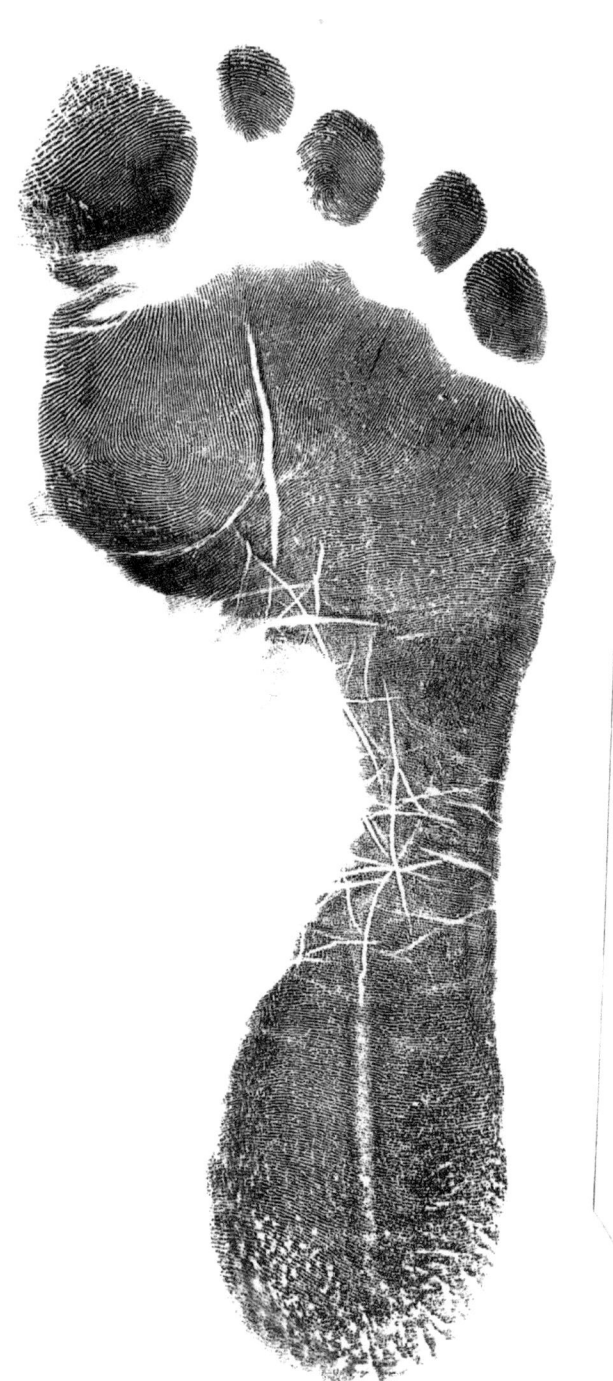

This is to certify that this is my foot print
6-09-95 x Michelle Brown
Print taken by _____

In Review:

There are several important discrepancies that are in question.

1. Michelle and I compared each other's Certificates of Birth given to our parents from Mary Immaculate Hospital in New York. Our footprints are on each certificate.

2. Cheryl's foot print is on Michelle's Certificate of Birth **BUT** Michelle's foot print is **NOT** on Cheryl's Certificate of Birth from Mary Immaculate Hospital. <u>If Michelle's foot print is not on Cheryl's certificate, than who does it belong to? This comparison was performed by the Covington Police Department, Covington, Georgia.</u>

3. Michelle's <u>time of birth was changed</u> from 3:15 to 3:22. Different inks were used. It is very obvious to see these changes.

4. Hospital birth certificates - Dr. Ryan's signature is signed in a totally different handwriting and style than on the letter he wrote our mother on November 20, 1951.

5. Dr. Ryan's signature is signed differently on the Coverslip certificates for Michelle and myself. He now used his full name.

6. There were three girls born in Mary Immaculate Hospital on January 15, 1951. Each baby was born two minutes apart from the other baby.

7. Ellen DiMatteo's birth certificate number is 401016. Time of birth is 3:25 pm. Was she the triplet born at 3:15?

8. Michelle Gemalo's birth certificate number is 401017. Time of birth is 3:22 Time of birth was changed from 3:15 to 3:22.

9. Cheryl Gemalo's birth certificate number is 401018. Time of birth is 3: 27

What do you think? <u>*The three of us know we are triplets.*</u>

Valid questions our mom had:

1. "Why did Dr. Ryan sign your birth certificates as the doctor at the time of birth when Dr. Travis actually delivered you girls?"

2. "Why were the birth names switched around? Michelle was named as the first born. I clearly stated that Cheryl was to be the **A** baby. Michelle was to be the **B** baby."

3. "During prenatal visits, three distinct heartbeats were heard."

4. "Dr. Ryan told me that he couldn't confirm or deny that you girls were identical or fraternal since one placenta can become fused with the other. However, after you girls were born, I was told that you were identical.

5. "No footprints were taken until I pressed the hospital nurses to take them. Since this is the case, my theory is as follows: Michelle was born first. <u>The identical twins followed.</u> Therefore, Cheryl has the identical, missing twin. <u>By mistake, they broke up the identical set of twins.</u> Therefore, Michelle and Cheryl are fraternal twins."

6. **"Please read pages 65 and 66 of this book regarding a meeting with our mom's friend, Maria. Maria was a psychic who also worked for the Suffolk County Police Department. Maria explains how our mother's third baby girl went "missing."**

*****

In 1985, I called Mary Immaculate Hospital and spoke with several nuns in administration. I told them that I would like to contact Dr. John P. Ryan. "Dr Ryan passed away a few years ago."

I asked, "Who took over his medical practice?" The nun replied, "His son, but he has retired from the practice. I don't know who took his place."

I did not want to hang up so I tried to think of something else to say to her.

"In the lower right corner of my birth certificate from the hospital, I see the name of the Superintendent, Sister Ursela Marie, O.P. Can I speak with her?"

"Oh no, Sister Marie passed away years ago too."

"Are there any records of our birth at the hospital?"

She replied, "No, several years ago there was a fire. All the microfilm records were destroyed." *How convenient, I thought! Another dead end.*

In Search of a Private Investigator - 1996

The years passed so quickly. Where did they go? In 1985, I married a wonderful man who happened to be an identical twin too. We traveled a lot and took amazing vacations together. Every weekend was an adventure. I loved being married again.

I continued to teach science in a middle school which was located in Covington, Georgia. I loved teaching. Raising my son, Matt and my daughter, Amy was also a blessing and a full time job! This took up so much of my time and thoughts over the years. I was fulfilled. Life was good.

However, time never stood still for me. Finding our triplet sister was a prayer that I wished for every day. I continued to interview several investigators. Whenever someone mentioned a "good one" I quickly made phone calls, hoping to find someone to assist us in our search.

Each investigator told me that they could not help us. They gave me lots of excuses. Many said, "It was not their field of expertise." I didn't realize how tough it would be to find a private investigator! I was given lots of advice. I made notes of all their suggestions. I even followed up a few, to no avail. Eventually I checked each one off my list. I guess they wanted an easy case to solve. I was beginning to understand that our case was far from the norm.

Interestingly enough, I had a friend who was able to help me find a very good private investigator. My friend, Marnie remains a good friend to this day. Our love of horses and riding together for hundreds of weekends kept us close.

Riding every weekend together kept us relaxed and sane. Our horses loved us as much as we loved them. The gentle four gaited beat of our Paso Fino horse's hooves touching the dirt was a rhythm that we loved to experience each weekend. I still yearn to be a part of a horse's life, even today.

Marnie's story is interesting, true and amazing. Without her, I would have never met her investigator, who became mine too. Our friendship was about to share more than the love of our horses.

One beautiful Saturday morning, while we were riding together I noticed that she was unusually quiet for most of our ride. Since this was not like her at all, I asked her if she was alright. As soon as I asked her that question, the floodgates opened. . *Riding will do that to you! It opens your heart and unleashes your inner most thoughts. It is cheaper than a psychiatrist and more fun too.*

As she wiped away the tears from her eyes, Marnie said that she wanted to share something with me. Something that she kept secret for almost thirty years. Her family nor her husband ever knew about her darkest moment.

She said, "Let's talk. I have something to ask of you and I know no one else that would understand." *I had no idea what she was about to share with me.* "Of course" I replied. "Let's stop for a few minutes and give our horses a break." She nodded her head as if to say, Ok." We walked our horses to a green, grassy spot under a very old Pecan tree which was close by. It provided us all with some much needed shade. As our horses gracefully chewed their luscious blades of grass, we dismounted and sat down under the same tree facing each other. I waited for her to begin.

"Oh Cheryl, please hear me out. You are the only person that can relate to my story." She lowered her head and whispered, "In 1970, I enrolled in a local college. In order to get there, I had to take the train. So each morning I walked about a half mile to the train station. On a Friday morning, a man took me totally by surprise and attacked me. He was so strong and deliberate. He dragged me into the bushes, stuffed a handkerchief into my mouth and raped me. He told me if I didn't fight him, he would not hit me in the face or hurt me. I will never forget his face or his crooked smile."

She tried to control her rage and her tears as she continued to say, 'I never took my eyes off him during the attack. I kept thinking that he looked familiar but I didn't know why."

"As he walked away from me, he turned around and gave me one last glance. I was so afraid to move. I sat there for a long, long time crying and not knowing what to do. The bushes were so thick and dense. No one even knew I was there."

Marnie was a little calmer and said, "I didn't go to school that day. I waited until it would have been time for me to return home. I walked into my parent's house as if nothing happened. I went upstairs, took a long, hot shower and remained in my room until the next morning. I never mentioned the attack to anyone. I guess it was my fault."

"Oh no, no it wasn't. He attacked you and violated you! If it wasn't you, he would have honed in on some other young girl." We hugged each other and we both cried.

After a few days, Marnie remembered that she saw him a few times on the train, just weeks before. He even talked to her several times. Marnie realized that this man was her attacker. He had been stalking her. Sadly, she soon found out she was pregnant.

Being raised as a Catholic, her parents made it very clear that she would never have their support if she had an out-of-wedlock child, no matter how it happened. This was an unwritten rule if you were raised in a family that chose anger and fear over love. My sister and I were told these exact words as teenagers too. *"The convent was always close by."*

In her seventh month of pregnancy, she found a home for unwed mothers. For the next two months she remained there until she gave birth to a baby girl. Knowing that she had no way of taking care of her baby, she gave her up for adoption.

Marnie's parents thought she was working at an out-of-town apprenticeship position in a school. During winter breaks, it was not uncommon for students to do this. Her parents never saw Marnie's growing belly, thanks to heavy sweaters, layers of clothes and bulky coats.

Now this is the coolest part of her story!

"Cheryl, I got a phone call this week while I was at work. It was from a private investigator. He informed me that my daughter, who was given up for adoption 28 years ago wanted to meet me! She found me and wants to meet me! What am I going to do? My husband doesn't even know that I was ever pregnant."

"Oh Marnie, just tell him. You didn't cause the attack. And you have a daughter! You have a daughter who wants to meet you. Chuck is a wonderful husband. He would never walk away from you. He trusts you and you trust him. Your marriage is strong." We bowed our heads and prayed for Marnie to have strength to tell her husband about her daughter. I smiled and said, "Chuck and Marnie now have a daughter. Cool."

That evening, Marnie told her husband about the phone calls with the private investigator. Chuck carefully chose his words and supported his wife in their new situation. He was not opposed to meeting Lisa. He was even excited that their family would now be blessed with a daughter.

During the next few weeks, Marnie spoke with her daughter, Lisa several times on the phone. Marnie was so afraid of meeting her alone at the airport. Marnie asked me if I would go with her to meet Lisa.

"Of course I'll go with you. I'll drive and you both can talk."

The reunion at the airport was wonderful. I was with Marnie when she first met her daughter, Lisa. They were both cordial and polite with each other. Marnie was afraid that Lisa would hate her for giving her up so easily. Of course that was not the case.

Since I was trying to find our triplet sister, I wanted to know if Lisa would tell me who her private investigator was. Without hesitation, Lisa gave me her P.I.'s e-mail address. I asked her how long she searched for her birth mother. She said, "three days." My heart skipped a beat. Maybe now I finally found a P.I. who worked with adoption agencies.

Our drive home from the airport was really interesting and fun. Lisa told me that her adoption was not sealed. Meaning, if she ever wanted to meet her birth mother, she would be able to contact her, and she did.

Both families had enough love in their hearts to share Lisa. She has two sets of wonderful parents. They are all closer now than ever. Their hearts are full. Life is good.

Over the next few years, Lisa married and both families became grandparents of two beautiful children.

Now I understood why Marnie said, "You are the only person who would understand my story."

Maybe we would be as fortunate as Lisa.

Maybe my sister and I will find our triplet sister.

****

Thanks to Marnie, I was able to call and hire her Private Investigator. I will call him "F." because he did not want to use his full name. We spoke many times and shared lots of important information.

In the following chapter, I will share with you his e-mail conversations and findings. The information is riveting. We were close, but not close enough.

****

I Hired a Private Investigator, F.

E-mails and our Conversations

May 5, 1997

When I called F., he was very skeptical of my intentions. He asked me not to use his real name, so we just called him "F." I told him how I obtained his name and number. He called Lisa to validate my story. To make sure I was "for real," he asked me to mail him a cover letter and our birth certificates. He asked me to mail them to a P.O. Box in New York City. Privacy was very important.

When F. finally called me back, he had a lot of questions. I did not have any answers to assist him. He spoke so quickly but I will never forget his words. **"Illegal adoptions were very common during 1950 – 1960 in New York. "Black market babies came with a high price. It was a lucrative business. I think I can help you girls, but it won't be easy. My sources work alone. It all takes time. I hope you are willing to be patient. I will do my best."**

He went on to say, **"It was easy to target welfare families, telling the birth mother that their baby had died in the hospital. Almost immediately afterwards, the child would be illegally sold-adopted to a family waiting for a baby. Some birth parents actually buried an empty casket."** These words were so upsetting to me. *It could have happened to us.*

I asked F. about our *coverslip certificates*. He confirmed that Michelle and I were definitely slotted out for adoption from Mary Immaculate Hospital. He didn't even flinch as he spoke these words.

He had seen coverslip certificates before. "They would be attached to the hospital certificate. No questions asked. You girls are lucky that you are still with your parents. Mary Immaculate Hospital had other plans."

If I had not been sitting down, I would have fallen to the floor. My body became weak and sad. He was so sure. He confirmed what we already knew to be true. *We did have a triplet sister who was adopted out. We were going to be next.*

Over the next few days, my investigator hit a lot of dead ends during his search for the truth. **"Illegal adoptions were protected under lock and key, more so than legal adoptions."**

F. knew people who could get into a *closed* file, but that was not the case for Michelle and me. He told me, <u>**"Your information about your triplet sister is well protected."**</u>

In an e-mail. He said, "Okay, so far I have checked and everything was okay with the Registry numbers." He went on to say, "I had one of my contacts do a search in the **NYC birth indexes** and yours and Michelle's names match the index numbers along with your birth sir name, Gemalo.

He told me what his costs were at that time. "He said, "The cost to me was $30.00. I also made two phone calls to two different sources to discuss your case. I had long distance costs which amounted to $6.00." *My goodness!*

He continued, "What I would like to do at this point is have this person do a full search of the year 1951 in the NYC birth index. The index is alphabetical, not by date or index number. They have quite a task at hand."

"Since this was a birth that they made legal, the index numbers should be close to yours and Michelle's. The first name may be listed for the child born. Since they wanted to legitimize the birth, the index numbers will be close"

He went on to say, "My source charges $200.00 for this service. It is a very time consuming process but this is what this person does. Let me know what you would like to do. I believe that this is the next logical step. Talk to you soon." *I was so excited.*

****

May 17, 1997

E-mail to me from F.

"Well, I went ahead and ordered a NYC date-of-birth search or voter registration, drivers and credit headers. It came back with two-hundred-eighty-seven women whose birth dates are January 15, 1951. The listing gives full names, addresses and the city. If we want to access an unpublished number, I know a P.I. who charges $150.00."

He also told me, "The data base search ran $125.00. I used the balance of the money I still had from you towards this cost. So, a balance of $40.00 is owed to me. I received confirmation that the person doing the index search for NYC has received payment. She gave me an approximate date of May 30th for the completion of their search of registry numbers."

He ended his e-mail by saying, "What do you think? I think we should probably talk first. I just don't want to be premature here." *I thought, "Let's go!"* Sincerely, F.

****

May 17, 1997

Conversation by phone with F.

F. and I spoke that same evening on the phone. I gave him the verbal green light to continue his search using his contacts. I would assume all costs to obtain any information regarding our triplet search.

****

June 4, 1997 E-mail to me from Michelle, my twin sister

Hi Cheryl,

I just got off the e-mail with F. He is a trip! East to chat with. He said, "Your birth # is **401018**. Mine is **401017**. There is a baby girl also born in Queens whose number is **401016**. He is going to trace her statistics through the Division of Motor Vehicles for hair color and body size/weight."

We had a good laugh because I told him it was privileged information what a woman's hair color and weight was. We Lie! Only our hair dresser knows for sure! I told F. we're 130+ depending on how social we were that week. He gave me a LOL response. That's the latest.

****

June 17, 1997

E-mail to me from F.

Cheryl,

These are the results from the NYC Birth Index Search.

Ellen DiMatteo	1/15/51 in Queens	#156-51-**401016**
Michelle Gemalo	1/15/51 in Queens	#156-51-**401017**
Cheryl Gemalo	1/15/51 in Queens	#156-51-**401018**
*Name With held	1/15/51 in Queens	# 156-51-401030
*Name With held	1/15/51 in Queens	#156-51-401077

***The two other births on that day were males.**

Notice that Ellen, Michelle and Cheryl have Birth Index numbers that are so close.

Our investigator, F continued, "Ellen DiMatteo. This is her birth name. We would have to try and track her down. Now, I did a state profile search of people born on 1/15/195. I found only one on this list with the name Ellen. The name listed was Ellen D. Vichnis. Many women retain **the initial of their surname when they marry, hence the Ellen D.**

"I investigated as high up on the ladder as I could go without blowing the whistle on myself. I was drawing attention to myself and others so I had to quit." He apologized several times and told me never to give up. "You'll find her if she wants to be found."

****

November 3, 1997   From F. to Cheryl

"I have not forgotten about you. I will keep you up to date s I hear something back from my source. I am at their mercy right now.

Sincerely,

F.

Three Girls Born at Mary Immaculate Hospital
On January 15, 1951

My private investigator was able to access birth records from January 15, 1951 at Mary Immaculate Hospital.

He told me that <u>there were three girls born in the hospital that day.</u>

Ellen DiMatteo was born in Mary Immaculate Hospital on January 15, 1951.

Her birth certificate number **is 401016.**

<u>Was Ellen born at 3:25 pm.?</u>   <u>(Was she the triplet born at 3:15?)</u>

Michelle Gemalo was Baby A. She was born in M.I.H. on January 15, 1951.

Her birth certificate number is **401017**.

Michelle was born at 3:22pm. **(Changed from 3:15)**

Cheryl Gemalo was Baby B. She was born in M.I.H. on January 15, 1951.

Her birth certificate number is **401018**. Cheryl
was born at 3:27 pm.

<u>**The birth certificate footprints of Michelle and Cheryl are also in question.**</u>

Michelle's Certificate Birth Certificate/Index Number is 401017

VR 115 (Rev. 6/87) 7-327006-350M   DOCUMENT NO. D079600

THE CITY OF NEW YORK
DEPARTMENT OF HEALTH
BUREAU OF VITAL RECORDS
CERTIFICATION OF BIRTH

This is a certification of name and birth facts on file in the Bureau of Vital Records, Department of Health, City of New York.

DATE OF BIRTH	JANUARY 15, 1951	CERTIFICATE NO.	156-51-401017
BOROUGH	QUEENS	DATE FILED	01-18-51
		DATE ISSUED	09-25-87

NAME   MICHELLE GEMALO ***

SEX   FEMALE

MOTHER'S MAIDEN NAME   JANE REDZISZ

FATHER'S NAME   STANLEY GEMALO

Irene A. Scanlon
IRENE A. SCANLON
CITY REGISTRAR

Do not accept this transcript unless it bears the raised seal of the Department of Health. The reproduction or alteration of this certification is prohibited by Section 3.21 of the New York City Health Code.

Cheryl's Certificate Birth Certificate/ Index Number is 401<u>018</u>

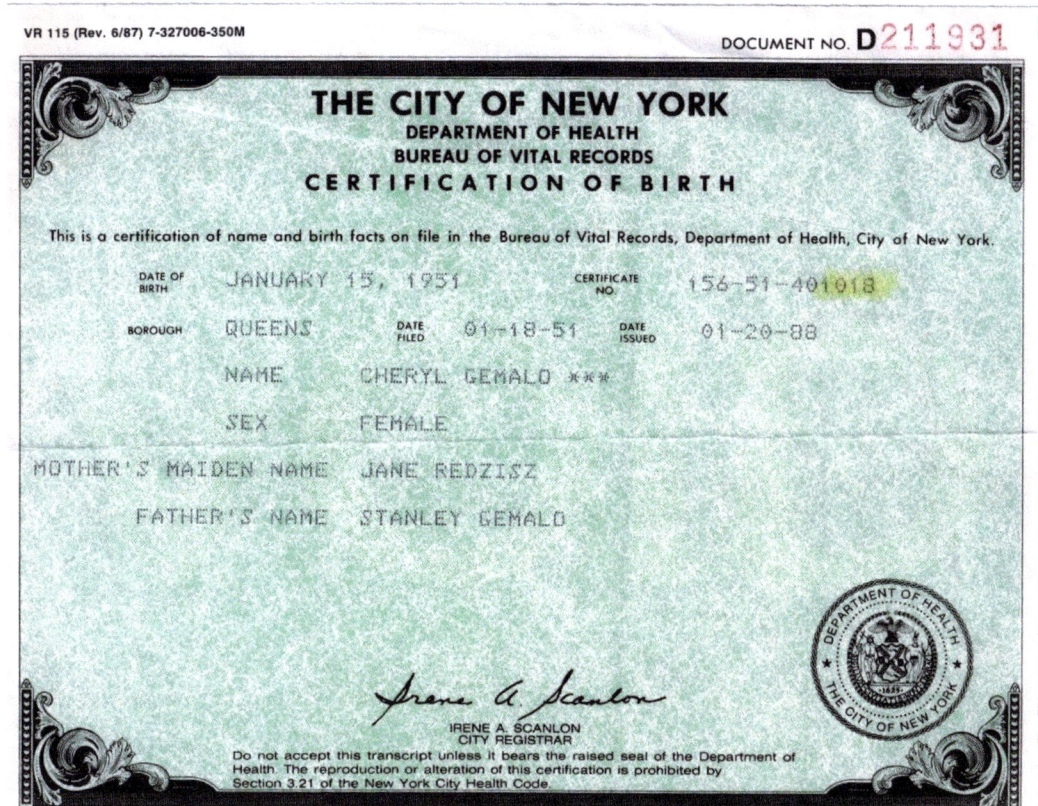

Final Thoughts

October 2017

Over these last ten years, Michelle and I have been told of many sightings. Of course, it always gets our hopes up. Unfortunately, none of them have helped us find our identical triplet sister.

In the front of this book, you can see the searches that we have been actively involved with. A lot of rejections had to do with our parents. They would not sign any disclosure agreements with any of the producers of any of the shows. However, since both of our parents are deceased, Michelle and I are free to look wherever we want to. At our age, there isn't much time left to look for our sister.

All in all, these rejections have given me the strength and courage to create my own book. Michelle and I are comfortable and blessed in our own lives. However, it sure would be wonderful to welcome our triplet sister into our family.

<u>I have so many unanswered questions.</u>

Has "Ellen" ever tried to find Michelle or me?

Were her parents preventing her from finding us?

Does she ever think about us, like we think about her?

Is she Michelle's identical twin or mine?

If she is worried about entanglements or legal implications, there are none.

We welcome this adult woman *and her family*, with open arms.

No Regrets.

Sincerely,

Cheryl and Michelle

Mom and her twin infants.

This is Michelle, Lynn and Cheryl. Our mother gave Michelle and me a perm!

Lynn is our friend who met our "identical triplet" so many times during the summer of 1963.

Michelle   Lynn   Cheryl

September 1959

First Day of 3rd Grade

Mom's Typed Story

December 14, 1987

Dear Chery,

I have just finished typing these 10 pages and I have to admit that it was not an easy job for me. Not having much typing experience, I did the best I could. It sure is easier reading then handwriting.

If there is anything that I left out please tell me as so much has happened over the years that it's just very difficult for me to remember it all. The story is fascinating at the very least and it sure holds your interest. As you can see I have changed the names of the doctors. Dr. Ryan is now Dr. Roan. Dr. Trivelino is now Dr. Travis. The hospital is Sacred Heart instead of Mary Immaculate. Al is now Abe. Everyone else is the same. These were *Leslie is Elizabeth* the only changes. Wouldn't it be something if Jeanette turns out to be a sister of yours and another daughter *Triplet?* of ours? What a hell of a story.

Many times during my writings I have gotten goose bumps and as a matter of fact I just got them again. The energy or something is still moving around. Keep it moving. Seeing this in writing is much more effective then just talking about it. So many coincidences. More then I ever realized. Wow this is really something. *(my son)* You will probably get this just about the time Matt *will* come home so be sure to say hello to him from us. Enjoy your visit you all, and have a very Merry Christmas. This New Year should be interesting to say the least. Bye for now and you all stay well.

Love,
Mom

P.S. *The brain moves quicker than the fingers.*

STILL SEARCHING
By Jane Gemalo

Certain names in this true story were changed for obvious reasons. The rest is the total truth from January 15, 1951 to the present time of 1987.

Not having slept too well last night, I decided to get up early and put my thoughts down on paper.

After the passage of almost thirty seven years this task is easier then I imagined it would be, as the experience is very much alive my mind. It feels like it happened only yesterday.

My water broke some time before 5:A.M. on the rainy and cold morning of January 15, 1951 and my husband took me to Sacred Heart Hospital where I was admitted to the labor room. This was in no way an easy pregnancy as I kept gaining weight at about ten pounds a month. My due date was to be some time at the very of February and by that December I had developed a serious kidney infection in my left kidney. X-Rays were taken and the doctor to me that I was pregnant with not only twins, but there was also a shadow of a third baby. At my next visit I was examined by a fema doctor who told me that she definitely heard three distinct heartl and to expect the birth of triplets.

At that time I was eighteen years old and who knew what was going My biggest mistake was to go through the Sacred Heart clinic. It was a nightmare and I bear the scars to this day. The worst part is that we had medical coverage through Eastern Airlines where my husband Stan was employed at that time, but were unaware of the coverage as it was a new thing at that time.

Each time I went, I was examined by a different doctor and was told the same story. "Be prepared for a multiple birth of at lea; twins." Here the story begins to unfold.

Six weeks before the due date, my water broke and I went into labor. After ten hours in the labor room, most of which time I was alone, I could feel one of the babies head begin to emerge. Screaming in agony a nurse finally came in and wheeled me into another room. This supposidly, was the delivery room.

Only at this time, was I given anything for the pain as this was a premature multiple birth, and did not know what happened in the until the following morning, when I finally woke up.

They gave me enough pain killers to knock out a horse.

While I was in labor, a young doctor came out to talk to my husband and told him to expect triplets. After the delivery there were only twin girls.

Once I awoke, it never dawned on me to question them as to what happened to the third child. I was given blood transfusions and was very weak and hurting terribly, and it was three days before they allowed me to see my babies, which had been placed in incubators. They weighted 4lbs. 11oz. and 5lbs. 5ozs. They were small, but they were fine and that's all that I cared about.

Shortly after giving birth, the question of names came up and we decided on Cheryl for Baby A and Michelle for Baby B. Much to my dissapointment they, the hospital people, reversed the names. Michelle was now Baby A and Cheryl was and always will be Baby B. Keep in mind, Cheryl was to be the name of the one born first.

I was very young and not at all very knowledgble in the ways of the world, as my twins were born twelve days before my nineteenth birthday, I was still only eighteen years old. They kept me in the hospital for ten days due to my weakened condition at which time I visited the nursery every chance I got. What I saw made me very uncomfortable. The nurses would prop up the baby bottles during feedings and if the baby moved, the bottle fell to the side and the baby just did not eat until the following feeding which was four hours away. This went on for an additional three weeks after my release from the hospital. My babies were just not thriving as three weeks later Michelle was down to 4lbs. 8ozs. + Cheryl 4lbs. 8½ ozs. That is a big weight loss for such a tiny baby. The were slowly but surely being starved to death.

My father decided that three weeks was long enough time, and much against hospital policy, we signed the babies out of the hospital. I at least wanted equal time.

Before we left with them, I insisted that they take footprints of the babies jusy in case of a mixup. This too was done very reluctantly. The original and only prints were given to me. They never bothered to keep a copy for themselves.

Once I got them home, I fed them around the clock and by Mid March their weight went up to 6lbs. 8ozs.and 6lbs.11ozs. Not bad for a young inexperienced mother, considering that I had no help with them whatsoever.

After about three days home, I removed the baby bracelets because they to me were very different and I was able to tell them apart. Even their cries were different.

This is when I began to questinn as to whether or not they were identical as I was told. To me they were not. Yet according to the hospital they were.

Birth Certificates were issued to each child and my doubts remained.

Within a few months we bought a house of our own in Babylon as we were living in a 2½ room apartment with hardly enough room to turn around in. The time was early April, and it was then that I wrote a letter to the hospital requesting more information from the doctor as to whether or not my twins were identical or fraternal.

As best as I can recall a doctor Travis delivered them, however a doctor Roan signed the birth certificates. Dr. Travis was at that time the head obstetrician of the hospital, and being that they were my first children, plus a multiple birth he decided to deliver them himself in case any problems arose.

An answer from Dr. Roan arrived stating that "as far as the findings go the twins were born in one placenta. However in some cases, two placentas become fused into one. Due to these findings, it can be assumed that the twins are identical."

To me they were always very different and in no way are they identical.

The doubt remained with me these many years and still does. Both girls are married and have two children each. Michelle has two girls and Cheryl has a boy and a girl. They are all very close in age. Less then a year apart. Cheryl was divorced and moved to Florida to be near Michelle and her family. While living in Florida she dated a man on the local police force named Al.

Here is where the story begins to unfold.

Cheryl lost a very good camera and reported it missing to the police for insurance purposes, and then, as with lost items forgot about it. In the meantime, a passage of perhaps two years, she re-married and moved to Ocala, to live there with her new husband.

Remember Al the police officer?

One night, Al had been out on a drug bust in which the suspect was shot and killed in his trailer. In the trailer the police found a great deal of stuff which looked to be stolen. Among the items was a camera. The same make of camera that Cheryl had lost. The police developed the film in order to get an idea as to whom the camera may have belonged. Keep in mind that in small towns every one knows everyone, especially young pretty women.

The film contained pictures of a pretty woman and two small girls about six years of age, perhaps twins.

From the developed film, Al immediately recognized Cheryl, her daughter and her neice. Al having no way to contact Cheryl, as she moved away and now had a different last name contacted us in Farmingdale, New York. He told us the story and I gave him Cheryl's new phone number in Ocala, where she could be reached. Al called Cheryl and explained to her that her camera had been found and that the film had been developed. Cheryl asked to see the pictures as she became curious as to Al's intentions. In a few days the pictures arrived, thats when the long distance wires began to buzz. She called me, greatly excited, as the woman in the pictures was not Cheryl but a girl who looked so much like her that she could have been her twin.

The resemblance was astuonding and I can understand very easily why
Abe [Al] thought that these were pictures of Cheryl. At first glance so
did we all. Her hair was worn slightly longer the our daughters
but the face was the same.

Could this be the missing triplet that appeared only on the X-Rays
then never materialized?

Pictures of this young woman appeared in the local newspaper under
the caption "Have you seen this woman?" The police thought that
the woman either was robbed of her camera or that she may have been
a victim of the man who was killed. No-one came forward to identify
her and to this day her identity remains a mystery.

Thirty six years have gone by, and my daughter Michelle was looking
for an apartment, and a real-estate woman came by to show her around
Michelle was shown a pretty apartment by a woman called Lizbeth
who kept staring at her during the tour. Lizbeth finally burst out
and said, "oh come on Jeanette, how long are you going to keep this
up? Stop pulling my leg. Michelle laughingly explained that her
name was not Jeanette but Michelle and that she must have mistaken
her for someone else. Lizbeth laughed too, still not believing her
and again said, "come on Jeanette, I've known you all my life and
you are definitely my first cousin. I cannot be mistaken. You're
playing a joke on me so come on that's enough. You know darn well
that we are cousins and have known each other all our lives, so
stop joking around.

By this time both women stopped joking around and started to take
one another seriously, and that something was wrong here.

You see, over the years, all of went to variousphychics, as something seemed to be missing from our lives. The phychics confirmed
our suspicions, but nothing definite was ever said. They touched
upon it then dropped it. Somewhere out there was another twin
who was also searching for something. You see, she is alone, my
girls have each other.

At one time several years ago, our daughter Paulette was working
for an Insurance company and the girls there kept telling her that
there was a girl working there also who looked very much like a
sister and were they related?

Paulette finally met this girl who by the way, looked very much like her twin sisters, and was their size, had frosted chin length hair the same color and whose name was Jeanette. Jeanette left the company in a very short time and came to Florida to work as a stewardess.

Paulette told us about this incident when she came home from work and we all just stared at one another.

Our three daughters are very lovely women and not at all average looking. More then once I have seen people turn their heads as they walked by, and more then once some smitten male bumped into a wall staring after them. They all are very unique looking, and as I said very lovely. Hardly the type you would run into every day. There have been other instances over the years where their paths have crossed. I am sure of it now.

One day, years ago, the twins went swimming to the local school pool. All the kids were splashin around having a good time in the sun when Michelle spotted Cheryl in the water and jumped on her back for a piggy-back ride. Someone who she thought was her sister but turned out to be someone else. Both girls were shocked when the girl said "I'm not Chery. The resemblance was great, but as kids go, they let the matter drop as they were perhaps thirteen at the time.

Again that nagging feeling came over me. Could there be something more to this? Could it be possible that the X-Rays and heartbeats were real?? Could I have had a child taken from me at birth without my knowing it? Did I give birth to triplets instead of twins? Was there another child?

Read on, it gets better as we go along.

Somewhere I remember reading, that the best time to visit a phychic was at the full of the moon or as close to it as possible, for best readings. We contacted Maria, a woman who is incredibly correct and whose predictions have been astounding in the past. My husband Stan came in with me to talk to Maria as we were there alone as it was early in the morning. Rather then sit in the car in the pouring rain Stan came in with me.

After the usual greetings, I looked at Maria and asked her to look way back in my past to 36 years ago when I was giving birth and to tell me what she saw. What went on at that hospital and how many babies did I give birth to.

7

Maria paused for a few long seconds staring at me and replied, "Isee a baby boy around you. Did you loose a boy at birth? I replid, not that I know of. She went on -----I see two rooms, You were moved into a room with another woman. Who was the woman in the same room with you? I see a great deal of money exchanged a family member is involved. A great deal of money. She claims that she saw me in a room with another woman whose baby boy had died at birth and one of my babies was given to her so she I assume would not go home empty handed. The spirit of that baby boy has attached itself to me and has been by my side for all these years.

Maria stopped talking for an instant, good thing, because we all three of us experienced a goose pimples, the likes of which you never saw. Our bodies were experiencing a reaction to some unknown force.

When we calmed down, Maria went on and told us to pursue this and not to give up the search. There is a third twin out there and destiny will bring us together. Our paths have crossed and we will seek one another out.

Ridiculous you think? Perhaps not.

My story is far from finished so lets get back to our fRiend Lizbet Michelle wanted to meet Jeanette as quickly as possible without arousing Lizbeths suspicions for this meeting. She did not want to rush Lizbeth because she was told that Jeanette had recently given birth and a few weeks time would be nice for Jeanette to get back on her feet. Lizbeth would set up a meeting as it was difficult for her to believe what she was seeing. Lizbeth was all for this meeting until she spoke to her mother about Michelle the exact duplicate of her cousin Jeanette. Lizabeths mother became furious and told Lizabeth to let it lay and not to interfere in her cousins family, and forget that you ever met Michelle. Jeanette is an adopted child who was never told about her adoption, and this would only open up an ugly can of worms. The entire family would be up in arms over this and to just forget the entire episode and to drop it right now.

I also fotgot to mention another thing that Maria told us about birth certificates, she said that you can easily change the month but not the year of birth. Jeanettes birthday is October of 1951 Our twins were born in January of 1951. Could a zero have been added to the one making it a 10? 1-51 to 10-51?

The possibility exists as a one can be changed to any number of month a 4 a7 a9 a10 an 11 or 12. Why nine months? Because it was the easiest?

SPECULATION Nine months from the day she got Jeantte her baby died? Why nine months? I also failed to mention prior to this that Jeanett was also born at Sacred Heart Hospital in Queens. Jeanettes adoptive parents now live in Maryland. Not far as miles go.

We'll skip over to another so called coincidence this one concerning Cheryl.

Just a few weeks ago Cheryl went to see a phychic just outside of Ocala. This is the first time she had gone to see this person so she did not know what to expect. As soon as she walked in the phychic said to her "Hello dear, how is your new baby doing? I only saw you a few weeks ago, how is everything? Cheryl was taken back and wantedto know more about this woman who looked so much like her, because she certainly was not this woman. This was her first visit there. Cheryl was very much surprised at this and wanted to know more about this woman who looked so much like her that she cold be her twin. The resemblance was that astounding.

FACT Michelle had never been to see this woman. Could this have been the elusive Jeanette?

Cheryl left her phone number with the phychic and asked her to please call her in case the woman came to see her again.

Not many people that we know of seek out phychics and fortune tellers. Could this woman be searching for something too?

Last year Cheryl went to get a passport because she was accompanying her husband on a trip out of the country. A birth certificate is required so she took hers down in order to get her passport. She was turned down because the birth certificate that I was given was not the original but a copy. There was no raised seal on it therefore it was not the original. For some reason I was never given the original but a copy.

We never knew we were given a copy until last year. Why did they give us a copy?

What were they covering up? Or is all of this just a set of strang circumstances?

My weight gain during the 7½ month pregnancy was 56lbs. After delive while at the hospital I weighted myself and I was down to my normal weight of 110lbs. The combined weight of my twins was an even 10lb The possibility of another placenta clearly exists.

Too many coincidences;

Jeanette born in Queens

Is an adopted child

Was never told she was adopted

Adoptive parents live in Maryland

Birth Certificates not original and never received the original.

Jeanette lives in Clearwater like the stewardess

Same year of birth, but in October

Twins not identical like I was told by the doctor

Names being turned around-Michelle being named the first born when I clearly stated Cheryl to be.

The idea of one placenta becoming fused with another, this information I have in writing from the doctor.

Why did Dr. Roan sign the certificates as the doctor at the time of birth when actually Dr. Travis delivered them?

The X-Rays of twins

The heartbeats of three babies

No footprints were taken of them until I pressed them to take them. If this is the case then my theory is that the now Michelle was first, and the identical twins followed.

Thefore Michelle has the identical missing twin. They by mistake broke up the identical set of twins. The girls are fraternal twins and not identical like I was told.

Truth is stranger than fiction, and if this is the case it is only a matter of time till the truth surfaces. You cannot keep somethin like this a secret forever. Someday, somehow, somewhere it will all come out. It is only a matter of time.

10

Before I close there is yet another coincidence not to be ruled out at this point. As far as I am concerned nothing is coincidental. Stan's sister is named Jeanette and my name is Jane. It was changed by the Immigration authorities from Jeanine to Jane because it was too difficult for them to pronounce.

Could they have named her Jeanette because they knew my name?

In Europe, Poland where I was born, these names are the feminine form of John, therefore, Jane is Jasha, and Jeanette is Jania.

As I stated-----It's only a matter of time.

If you pinch hard enough, Somewhere along the line someone will begin to squeak.

We are talking abuot a serious offense which would be called kidnapping.

As the title states, we are STILL SEARCHING, and will continue to do so until we meet again.

We all have unusual first names;
Cheryl
Michelle
Paulette
Jeanette — triplet?
Jeanine — mom

Our Parents, Stanley and Jane Gemalo

Dad passed on September 2, 1997. Mom passed on May 13, 2005.

Michelle and I promised our mom, we would never stop looking for "her."

If the following story had not happened to me, I probably would not have believed it either. I called it, **I Think My Best Friend is Your Identical Twin** because of someone that I met in November of 1994. I know it is a long story, but all of it is true. **This is Wanda's story.**

November 29, 1994
Conyers, Georgia

I Think My Best Friend is *Your* Identical Twin

On a chilly and brisk afternoon, I went to Eckerd's on Hwy. 138 to refill my daughter's prescription. An attractive woman with a happy personality, who I had never met before, assisted me at the pharmacy counter.

On December seventh, I returned to Eckerd's to pick up the rest of Amy's medication. As I was writing out my check, the same woman who I met previously said to me, "I know your twin."

I looked up at her and my eyebrows lowered in deep thought. *I know the last time Michelle was with me in Eckerd's was in May. Could this woman have such a good memory? She knew Michelle?*

Shaking my head in doubt, I said, "The last time my sister visited my family was before the summer and…"

Wearing a full smile, the woman behind the prescription said, "No, no, not here. Your twin is in Wyoming. You have an identical twin who lives in Wyoming." I asked, "Why did you say that" How do you know her:" "She is my best friend." Replied the jovial woman.

"When I first met you a few days ago, I thought you were my friend from Wyoming, coming to surprise me in Conyers. She travels a lot. I knew it was her."

I wanted to hear her mention her best friend's name, but she didn't. I thought, "Ears, don't fail me now." I couldn't move. *Could this really be happening? Maybe I would finally find our triplet sister?*

I stopped writing my check. I had to lean on the counter. At that moment, I needed support to hold me up. I felt overwhelmed with emotion. I wanted to tell this woman all about my private search, yet I was in the center of the Eckerd's pharmacy counter. People were waiting in line behind me, listening to our conversation.

I tried to contain myself and stay calm. On the inside, I was elated and overcome with excitement for the chance to follow any lead that might end my life long search, for the sister that we know is out there.

I immediately thanked my guardian angel for providing me with this opportunity, an opportunity that I had been waiting for. I tried to mentally visualize my angel but all I could see was a shadow over my left shoulder.

I tried to focus. I took a slow, deep breath. Inside, my mind was racing. I energetically but cautiously told this kind woman, whom I had never met before, "I have been searching for our identical, triplet sister. She was separated from us at birth, for reasons which remain a mystery."

I continued, "I don't care about the reasons why she was given up for adoption. Michelle and I are not out to blame anyone for the separation. There are no right or wrong reasons anymore. The past is the past. Hopefully, the future would include our triplet sister."

I sighed and said in a whisper of a voice, "Until then, I will never stop looking for the girl that we met at the Farmingdale pool in 1963. I will always feel as if a part of me is missing."

Many thoughts raced through my mind. My younger life flashed before my eyes as if I was seeing a slide show of still moments. I recalled the many times the three of us met as children at the pool and in Mid-Island Plaza.

I asked the very happy clerk what her name was. It was Wanda. Wanda wanted to hear more about our triplet search. So I said, "Each time that we met at the public pool, we sat so close to each other on the cement. We were too shy to speak, all three of us.

Meeting her became so easy and comfortable. Personally, I thought that we would always meet again. Michelle and I talked to each other about the movie called Parent Trap with Haley Mills. We really thought that our meeting was supposed to be this way, just like in the movies! It never occurred to us that the meetings would come to an end. How naïve we were. We were children."

Since childhood, we never met again. We've had many reminders from other people that claim to have met her. The occurrences are many. They are all written down and kept in a binder that I labeled, The Triplet Search."

As Wanda and I talked and listened to each other in amazement, we never seemed to take our eyes off each other. I asked Wanda, "How do you know her? How did you meet?"

She easily said, "We are both adopted. She is Fern Foster's adopted niece. We share that commonality. She knows nothing about her past. Wanda shrugged her shoulders.

"Who is Fern Foster?"

Wanda didn't answer although I know she heard me.

I wanted to ask her to take a break to come outside and continue our conversation. I didn't mention this because my sixth sense told me that she might resist any deep discussion; so I tried to keep it light.

Wanda continued to check out other customers while speaking to me at the same time. Her bright, sparkling eyes were dancing with the confidence that I wish I felt too. To acquire more information, I asked her what her friend's age was.

"Well, I was born in 1953. She is two years younger than me."

I waited for Wanda to continue. I was in shock. Wanda thought for a moment and said with a smile, "I'm 41 and that makes her 39."

"When is your friend's birthday? Ours is January 15, 1951. We were born six weeks prematurely though. We are also 39."

Wanda seemed to ignore my question regarding her friend's birthday, but she still smiled and shook her head in disbelief. I know she heard me. She seemed to just stand there in a haze, looking right at me.

Having this new information, I wanted to collapse right there on the spot! *Could this be how we'll all meet? Is this really happening?* I thought.

I lowered my head, trying to get a grip on my emotions while trying to use my time wisely. After all, Wanda was in the middle of working at the pharmacy counter. It was a busy place, this time of year.

I didn't want to monopolize her time. I didn't want to leave either. My feet were glued to the same spot. I had so many questions to ask. I pushed on and asked, "May I call her? Do you have her phone number?"

She immediately interrupted me for the first time in a protective, negative manner and said, "No. I'll call her. I want to tell her myself. I don't know how she'll take this. She comes from a very well-to-do family. Let me talk to her first."

Wands continued to look down and sort out prescriptions to be filled. Her unexpected bluntness shocked me. I felt as if I had just been slapped. I felt confused. I felt as if I was guilty of intruding into someone's life, entering without permission as if to cause harm to a loved one. All of a sudden, I was embarrassed to be there, in front of all these waiting, sick customers. I wanted to snap my fingers and vanish into thin air. But, I'm not the one who brought up this subject, so I shouldn't feel as if I was being intrusive.

I thought, *"Was I at the right place at the right time?* I wasn't sure anymore. Our discussions were very private and sensitive. And here we were, discussing it over a counter, in public no less. I think I had everyone's ears, yet people acted as if they didn't hear me. I wanted to disappear.

To neutralize the tension between us, I took a deep breath and quietly said, "Someone (Dr. Harrison, a physic in Ocala, Florida) told me to be patient. She would not want to meet us, at first. It naturally would be a shock and an unbelievable surprise to her. She would not want to upset or alienate her adopted family. To her, we were intruders." *We felt differently.*

Dr. Harrison continued. "It will take her time to digest what Michelle and you have become comfortable living with for the last thirty years."

Wanda shook her head in agreement and continued to work. Her defensive guard came down. She was once again calm and gentle. Wanda understood what I was saying. I was no longer a threat to Wanda and her best friend.

She looked around the store several times. I knew that my time here was almost over. I had to let her do her job. I had to leave.

In order to unglue my feet, I had to recap some information so as not to doubt my own ears. I wanted to validate my sanity; to make sure I was not making any of this stuff up.

"When you call her, will you please give her my phone number so we can talk?" I felt as if I was pleading and begging for my life to be spared. She looked for a pen and paper and wrote my phone number down as she nodded her head in assurance to my request.

"Let me talk to her first. Don't get your hopes up. Just let me talk to her first."

Sadly, I prepared myself to leave. I had the courage to ask Wanda one more question. "If someone had told you, knowing that you are adopted too, that you were genetically part of a twin set, wouldn't you want to meet them?"

As she looked down at me smiling, she said something which sent a bolt of positive energy, like lightening through me. "She's energetic, like you."

I felt connected in a strange way to Wanda. I didn't want to leave, wondering if I would ever see her again.

"Are you sure? I mean… look at me. How do you know for sure?" I said sheepishly. She continued to make eye contact with me and said, "Cause I am looking at her right now. I'm looking at her!"

All I saw was her positive smile. All I heard was her voice. Everything else was nonexistent. I tried not to get my hopes up.

With that delicate news of encouragement, my soul illuminated with a radiant inflorescence. I felt warm all over. I felt my cheeks flush with heat. Inside my head, I tried to quiet the joyful screams of relief that I felt. I was hoping that no one else saw my trembling hands, which I quickly tucked deep inside my jacket pockets.

So, very casually, I happily told Wanda that I would await her call. I was hoping we would be able to have our reunion talk on that very night.

I knew it was time for me to leave the store counter. I said, "Bye Wanda. I look forward to hearing from you soon. Meeting you is a dream come true."

I walked out of Eckerd's slowly, trying not to show my fragile, excited state of being to anyone. I was trying to soak in all that I had just heard.

I couldn't wait to share my news with my sister, Michelle so I phoned her as soon as I got to my car. Circuits were busy. *Should I be surprised?* I could not get through to Florida! Then I called home and spoke to my daughter, Amy. I tried to tell her what just happened. My mind kept racing. I couldn't stand my inability to think. This was not like me, so I mentally cooled down in the privacy of my car. It was 6:30 at night.

I asked my guardian angels to relax the energy in me and to give me patience. In this state of mind, I was of no use to anyone. I certainly would not drive until I felt calm again.

While driving home in darkness, I was glad to be alone with my thoughts. Yanni's, <u>Private Collection</u> taped-music helped me disperse my excitement. Somehow, I reached my garage, parked my car and opened the door to the kitchen. I tried to walk in as if this sort of thing happens every day.

I told the full story to my husband, Ray and my daughter, Amy. They were both full of smiles and support. How lucky I was to have this family. Ray advised me not to get my hopes up.

I called my twin sister. We seemed to hug each other over the phone. Was this too much to ask for? We hoped not.

I also phoned our younger sister, Paulette. She is thirty-two. We were both out of our minds with joy. The facts that we shared, were too many to be just another coincidence. And believe me, over the years there have been many. Waiting would be the difficult part.

Paulette said, "You've waited all these years, what's a few more days."

****

A few days passed without receiving a phone call from Wanda. So, after work, I drove to Eckerd's again, as if I had one mission in mind, and I did. I walked over to the pharmacy counter and asked to speak to Wanda. She was working. I was so relieved to see her.

We gave each other a friendly, "Hello." She seemed happy to see me too. I quickly got to the point and said, "Wanda, did you make the phone call to your friend?"

She said, "I left a message on their answering machine. They weren't home. Maybe they went away for the Christmas holidays."

My heart sank but at least I knew that Wanda's efforts were real. I then took the opportunity to ask Wands for her phone number. I asked her if I could take her to lunch sometime soon. We both agreed that that would be nice.

Before I left, I asked Wanda, "Do you still feel the same after meeting me three times?"

She smiled again and said, "Yes."

Then she surprised me and said, "You'll meet… and then the next time, it will be my turn."

I think she wanted to find her entire family too. I promised to share any information that I had, regarding how to find a loved one. We both parted friendly. It felt wonderful.

****

Several days passed without hearing from Wanda. I phoned her several times. Finally one afternoon, someone answered the phone. I asked to speak to Wanda. She told me that she was out shopping. Happily, Wanda returned my call a few hours later.

At first, she acted as if she didn't know who I was. We made small talk until she remembered who I was. *Strange.*

I gently opened up the conversation by saying, "I didn't want to speak to you in front of the pharmacy counter. That is your place of employment. I was hoping we could talk now."

I asked Wanda to tell me anything about her friend. Her guarded response was, "What do you want to know?"

"Well, there are a few questions. Does she have the same hair color? Does she like horses? Does she like cooking? Is she the same weight? Does she have the same square teeth that I do? Was she ever married? Does she have any children besides the daughter that you mentioned to me previously?"

Wanda patiently answered, "Yes, she looks like you but she has darker hair. She wears it very long, down past the middle of her back."

I replied, "Well Michelle and I highlight our hair several times a year. We have darker hair also."

"You're kidding. Oh no! Her hair is beautiful. She is a fabulous dresser. She goes to rodeos, but then everyone in Wyoming does. She is a wonderful homemaker and cook. She is the same weight and she does have square teeth!" She laughed at the end of her descriptions.

We both chuckled and went on to discover much more "crossed" information about each other.

Wanda continued, "She had been married to Arnold (Arnie) Mock in a small town in Wyoming. He was a president of a bank. Arnie and Jack (Wanda's husband) were close friends. They grew up together.

About twelve years ago, in 1982, Arnie was killed in a plane crash."

At that point, I said, "Wait!" *I had to interrupt her and finish her story because I knew it.*

"Was the plane a small, private plane?"

Wanda said, "Yes."

"Did it go down and crash due to ice on the wings?"

Again, Wanda said, "Yes."

"Did Arnie and three work associates die in that crash?"

"Yes."

I then went on to say, "The men had a choice to take a commercial airline, but chose the smaller plane instead. They thought it would get them all home quicker. Is this correct?"

"Yes."

Wanda asked, "How do you know this?"

"Well, I went to a physic reader in 1986. He told me that this crash would happen to *my* husband, Ray. My husband would die in a small plane crash due to icing on the wings. All men would perish. My husband would die in the height of his career." I heard nothing but silence.

"My husband is the president of sales and marketing for The Closet Maid Corporation. Their executives fly to Canada, Colorado and Las Vegas using the company Lear Jet, several times a year."

Wanda gasped.

I took a deep breath and continued.

"I begged my husband not to take the Lear Jet home from one of his Colorado, wintery trips. He trusted me enough to book a flight with a commercial airline. The physic also told me that I would be left financially well off, with a lot of money in deferred stocks and bonds. I would not marry for many years though." *Of course, I didn't tell Ray that.*

"Thank God, Clairson's Lear Jet never crashed. All men returned home safely. I am so sorry that Arnie's plane did not. Gosh, I think my physic read "your friend" instead of me. If she is my triplet sister, this isn't unusual. It's happened to Michelle and me many times. Our physic readings overlap lot."

Silence

Wanda added, "Loosing Arnie was very rough on her. My friend was far enough along in her pregnancy. She was pregnant with a baby girl. She stayed single for many years, until she remarried. Now she is doing great. Very wealthy and happy. She has another child now." *Whew.*

"What brought you to Georgia?"

She said, "My husband and I had enough of cold winters in Wyoming. I was born in Georgia. My family had eight children. The kids were adopted out to other families. I was adopted in Wyoming. I also have a sister named Paulette. I have a brother who lives near Marietta, Georgia. I haven't seen him in eight years. My grandmother lives in Athens. She's dying."

I felt as if I had a new friend in Wanda. I told her that I would be more than happy to go with her to visit her brother and grandmother, since she and Jack only had one car. If she needed me to help her, I'd be there.

"Wanda, you are not alone. Even if your dear friend in Wyoming might not be ready to be my sister yet, maybe you and I can still remain friends."

Wanda appeared to be deep in thought and eventually said, "Ok."

Then she added "I met my birth mother once, a few years ago."

"Why don't you want to add her and the family into your life?"

Her reply was, "I'm afraid. I don't want to open up a can of worms."

I didn't want to bring any negative thoughts or energy to our conversation so our conversation came to an end. She told me she would call her best friend again soon. I reminded Wanda that Ray and I were traveling for the holidays also. We would not return until December twenty-sixth.

"No problem. We'll talk soon."

****

In early December, I returned to Eckerd's to chat with Wanda once more. She no longer worked there!

"What?" I thought.

"Where did she go? Did she leave a forwarding phone number?" The clerk was sorry. She couldn't give out that private information to me. *Would I ever see Wanda again? She left me with so many unanswered questions. How could she do this to me?*

My heart was heavy as I walked out of the store. When I got to my car, I tried to call the phone number that she gave me a few days ago. I was told, "Wanda and Jack no longer lived there." Again, they would not give me any forwarding information. **This is not fair. I cried.**

****

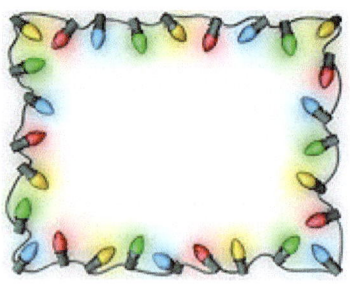

January 1994

I did receive a short letter from Wanda. She wrote to me on January 15, 1994. That happens to be our birthday.

In the letter she said, "How are things in Georgia? Hope all is well with your family. I have not heard from Patsy. I hope we will return to the south. It is damn cold up here." Her return address showed that she lived in Green River, Wyoming.

When school let out for the summer, I finally had time to write Wanda a letter. She never got to read it. It was returned to me, unopened.

The envelope read, Return to Sender. No Forwarding Address. *Another dead end?* I was so upset.

At least I know her complete name is Wanda Wilson. She also mentioned her best friend, Patsy's name. (If that's really her name.) For the last twenty years, I thought our triplet's name was Ellen D. Who knows? Maybe it is.

2017   ****

Twenty-three years have passed since I last heard from Wanda Wilson. I never heard from her best friend and identical twin of mine, Patsy. <u>Still Searching</u> is dedicated to our mother.

"The truth has a way of finding you…"

I hope…

Cheryl Kaye and Michelle Ritson 2016

Michelle Ritson 2017

Michelle Ritson and Cheryl Kaye 2017

Cheryl Kaye 2017

Michelle Ritson and Cheryl Kaye   November 2017

Printed in Dunstable, United Kingdom

74177828R00049